NOW I REMEMBER

By the same author

*

FREDERICK THE GREAT

PENDLEBURY AND THE PLASTER SAINTS
(with Colin Badcock)

BUDGE FIRTH—A Memoir and Some Sermons
(Editor and part author)

A HOLIDAY HISTORY OF FRANCE
A HOLIDAY HISTORY OF SCOTLAND
SUMMER PILGRIMAGE
THE PLUSCARDEN STORY

NOW I REMEMBER

A Holiday History of Britain

by

Ronald Hamilton

CHATTO & WINDUS

THE HOGARTH PRESS

LONDON

Published by
Chatto & Windus Ltd
The Hogarth Press
40 William IV Street
London WC2N 4DF

For JAY
with love and thanks

First published 1964
Reprinted 1973
New edition 1983

British Library Cataloguing in Publication Data

Hamilton, Ronald
Now I remember: a holiday history of Britain.
—New ed.
1. Great Britain—History
I.   Title
941   DA32

ISBN 0 7011 2669 8

Printed in Great Britain by Martin's of Berwick

THE OBJECT

The object of this little book is not to *teach* but to *remind*.
I have been driven to it by questions asked by my family
which expose the inadequacy of my memory. We have all
been taught History, the trouble is that we have all forgotten. We go about the countryside, we look at churches,
castles and houses, we are quite good at "Norman", "Early
English", "Decorated", "Perpendicular", etc., but we find
ourselves saying: "Who was on the throne then?"; "How
did Henry IV succeed Richard II?"; "What *was* Henry
VII's claim to the crown, and who *were* the Beauforts?"

I have tried to answer these questions, under architectural
periods. You are not asked to master anything new, you are
merely reminded of facts which were once familiar. Put the
book in your pocket or throw it into the car. If it increases
the enjoyment of your drives and of your holidays, it has done
what it set out to do.

RONALD HAMILTON

Acknowledgments

The sources of the photographic illustrations in this book are all acknowledged individually, and I am grateful to those who have given me permission to reproduce them.

The line drawings illustrating a typical dress of each reign are the work of Miss M. T. Ritchie, who prepared them specially for this volume.

I wish to express my thanks for being allowed to quote from the following:

> *Henry VIII* by A. F. Pollard. (Longmans, Green & Co. Ltd.)
>
> *History of England* by G. M. Trevelyan. (Longmans, Green & Co. Ltd.)
>
> *Queen Victoria* by Lytton Strachey. (Chatto and Windus Ltd.)
>
> *A King's Story*, The Memoirs of H.R.H. The Duke of Windsor, K.G. (Cassell & Co. Ltd.)
>
> A Letter in *The Times* of 20 March 1963 from Dr. G. R. Elton.

Many friends have helped me with advice and the loan of books, etc. Miss Mary Pettman of the National Portrait Gallery, Miss Alethea Hayter, Mrs. Carpenter-Turner, Miss Joanna Lubbock, and Mr. A. W. Kerr. I am particularly indebted to Mr. B. W. Robinson of the Victoria and Albert Museum, to Miss Ursula Hamilton, and to Dr. Peter Partner and Mr. Ruthven Hall – both of Winchester College.

Above all I wish to thank my secretary, Miss F. M. Bartlett, who has seen the whole job through all its stages.

R. H.

The College,
Winchester

Contents

NORMAN
1066–1189

Photograph by Sydney W. Newbery

NORMAN
Waltham Abbey, the Nave looking East
(By permission of Pitkin Pictorials, Ltd.)

NORMAN

1066–1189

The style of architecture which we, in our insular way, call "Norman" is known elsewhere in Europe as "Romanesque" ("l'art roman", the French call it). There is no harm in your working on the dates which I give above; they will do, but no dates of architectural periods can ever be accurate, and, in fact, "Norman" architecture was introduced into this country before the Norman Conquest, and went on after the five Norman kings.

Once the Normans had established themselves, and things had settled down, there was an enormous amount of building. Churches bigger than the biggest in Normandy sprang up, village churches were pulled down and replaced; it was an astonishing feat in a land of which the population, under William Rufus, probably numbered less than two million.

The Norman style is easy to identify. You go into a church and you see round (or semi-circular) arches. The walls are thick, the windows are small, and the whole is supported by great, fat cylinders of pillars. There may be rich ornamentation on the arches: rope, foliage, zig-zags (these terms explain themselves), but the general impression is one of solidity and toughness – admirably exemplified by Waltham Abbey. Such is a Norman building.

SOME 'NORMAN' MOULDINGS

NORTH HINKSEY, BERKS. PATRICKSBOURNE, KENT

ROMSEY, HANTS.

Photograph by R. Lécluse (Falaise)

Statue of William the Conqueror at Falaise

WILLIAM THE CONQUEROR, 1066–1087

Born 1027, was 39 in 1066, and 60 when he died.

Married Matilda, daughter of Baldwin of Flanders. Had four sons:

> Robert, Duke of Normandy
> Richard (killed hunting)
> WILLIAM II (Rufus)
> HENRY I

and five or six daughters – including Adela, who married Stephen, Count of Blois.

Thumbnail Sketch   A pious, clean living, courageous soldier and an able, ruthless administrator.

WHAT TO REMEMBER

Edward the Confessor (1042–1066) spent nearly thirty years in Normandy before he was recalled to England to succeed Harthacnut. He prepared the way for the Conquest by putting Normans in high places, by practising a monkish chastity which deprived England of an heir of his body, and, perhaps, by nominating as his successor William of Normandy, his first cousin once removed. On his death bed, however, his choice switched to his brother-in-law Harold, a selection which was confirmed by the Witan, the council of the Anglo-Saxon kings.

But Harold laboured under a disadvantage burdensome to the medieval mind. Finding himself a constrained guest at William's court in 1065, he had forsworn the English throne – an oath rendered the more impressive by reason of its having been made upon a formidable collection of relics. In addition, Pope Alexander II was anxious to force a stricter ecclesiastical discipline upon this country and was prepared to support the installation of Duke William in order to further this end.

Nevertheless, on the Confessor's death, Harold accepted the crown, and put himself and his troops in a state of invasion alert. He was first tested in the North, whither he had to march against Harold Hardrada of Norway, whom he beat at Stamford Bridge on 25 September 1066. Three days later William landed at

Pevensey, backed by the lofty sanction of the Papacy and a well-trained force, and defeated the gallant but war-weary Harold on 14 October at Hastings, an engagement which Sir Edward Creasey justifiably included in his "Fifteen Decisive Battles of the World". William then moved to London and was crowned at Westminster on Christmas Day. Opposition, which continued in various areas, was ruthlessly crushed – one remembers, particularly, The Harrying of the North (1069) and the defeat of Hereward the Wake (1070–1072).

The years which followed saw the riveting of Norman-type feudalism upon England – everybody, right down the hierarchy, was the King's man first and foremost (Oath of Salisbury 1086) – and, except on the marches, where considerations of defence were paramount, no noble had a large holding of land in any one area. With this went the replacement of Saxon ecclesiastics by competent and cultivated Normans (e.g., Lanfranc for Stigand at Canterbury) and the reinforcement of Church Courts – all of which brought England more into the stream of continental life than had hitherto been the case. In order to facilitate taxation William instituted a survey which culminated in the production of Domesday Book (1085) – a brilliant administrative document and a memorial to the fact that the Anglo-Norman monarchy was the strongest in Europe.

"The English flee at Hastings", Bayeux Tapestry

William II, Great Seal, Eton College
(*By permission of the Provost & Fellows of Eton College*)

WILLIAM II (RUFUS), 1087–1100

(Son of WILLIAM THE CONQUEROR)

Born 1056, was 31 when he ascended the throne, and 44 when shot dead by an arrow in the New Forest (? Walter Tirrel). Unmarried.

Thumbnail Sketch   "Nasty, brutish and short."

WHAT TO REMEMBER

It is probably true, though difficult to believe, that the Conqueror preferred William Rufus to his other sons. Certainly it was his will that Robert, the elder, should become Duke of Normandy, and William King of England, with the result that the latter, having made numerous fair promises (a practice at which he became adept in times of crisis or illness), was crowned at Westminster on 26 September 1087. A powerful group of barons, no doubt thinking that life would be more agreeable under the easy-going elder brother, rose in his favour on grounds of primogenital right. William turned astutely to the native English, made lavish guarantees of good government, and secured help adequate to suppress the rebellion. Once his position was established he observed cynically: "Who is there that can fulfil all that he promises?"

There followed a campaign in Normandy, where William achieved a firm foothold, and some successful operations against the Scots, which also served to increase his power in the north of England. In 1089 a fever struck down Lanfranc, who had advised William well, and the King became increasingly extortionate and tyrannical. His chaplain and adviser Ranulf Flambard, who later became Bishop of Durham and to whom we owe much of that incomparable cathedral, was quick to appreciate the financial advantage of keeping the see of Canterbury vacant and diverting its revenues into the royal coffers. Handsome profits were made until an illness in 1093 put William in fear for his immortal soul, and led to the hasty appointment, as Archbishop, of the noble and saintly Anselm, Abbot of Bec.

William recovered to enjoy another piece of good fortune in

1096, when his brother Robert, inspired to take part in the First Crusade and needing money, pledged Normandy to him in return for ready cash and gave him an opportunity for another visit to the continent, and for further successful military operations. Meanwhile Anselm, who had made a bad start with the King by subscribing a mere five hundred pounds towards the Normandy expedition of 1094 ("Keep your money and your jaw to yourself; I have enough of my own. Get you gone", said Rufus), found himself increasingly involved in disputes with his royal master, and departed wearily to Rome in 1097, whereupon the latter gleefully seized the archiepiscopal estates.

This reign, of twelve horrible years, came to an end on 2 August 1100, when the King, hunting in the New Forest, was killed by an arrow. Nobody will ever know whether this was an accident or whether his companion, Walter Tirrel, who left swiftly for foreign parts, was one of England's benefactors.

Photograph by A. W. Kerr

Tomb of William Rufus, Winchester Cathedral

Henry I, Silver Penny
(By permission of the Trustees of the British Museum)

HENRY I (BEAUCLERC), 1100–1135

(Son of WILLIAM THE CONQUEROR, brother of WILLIAM RUFUS)

Born 1068, was 32 when he ascended the throne, and 67 when he died.

Married Matilda, daughter of Malcolm III of Scotland, herself descended in the direct line of English kings before the Conquest, from Egbert. Had one son, William, drowned in the "White Ship" 1120, and one daughter, Matilda, who, aged eleven, married Henry V, the Holy Roman Emperor (which means, approximately, "Germanic Emperor"), in 1114. Henry I's Queen Matilda died in 1118 and, in 1121, the King married Adelaide, daughter of Godfrey of Louvain, wishing to have a son. No success.

Thumbnail Sketch   Firm, businesslike, educated, "The Lion of Justice."

WHAT TO REMEMBER

Henry Beauclerc was also following the hunt when Rufus died. Exploiting the absence of his eldest brother Robert on the crusade, he rushed to Winchester and seized the royal hoard. The Anglo-Saxon chronicle records that, after Rufus' burial, "the Witan who were then near at hand chose his brother Henry as King, and he . . . then went to London".

It was desirable to win immediate popularity. Henry imprisoned Flambard, recalled Anselm, married a princess of the English line and granted a charter calculated to please all classes. This policy paid, and the English remained loyal when Robert, back from Palestine, landed at Portsmouth in 1101. Peace was made, without military action, and Robert returned to Normandy, mollified by a substantial pension and acknowledging Henry's right to the English throne. But there were overmighty subjects who favoured Robert, and these Henry suppressed until "no man in England dared to rebel or hold any castle against him". But lasting peace was impossible with Robert a free agent, so Henry crossed the channel and defeated his brother at

Tinchebrai on 28 September 1106, a celebration of the fortieth anniversary of the Conqueror's landing at Pevensey which delighted the English infantry engaged and made Henry master both of Normandy and England.

Henry also showed statesmanlike skill during seven years of negotiation with the high-principled and obstinate Anselm over the matter of investitures. The Archbishop had returned a convert to the view of Hildebrand (Pope Gregory VII) that the appointment of bishops and archbishops (called their "investiture") was a matter for the Church, not for the King. This was a serious challenge to a monarch when great ecclesiastics were also powerful feudatories. Eventually a compromise was achieved at Bec, in Normandy, in 1106, whereby the papal side allowed prelates to do homage to the King, while Henry forewent all claim to invest with ring and staff – to him the conferring of spiritual authority mattered little, whereas feudal sovereignty was of vital importance.

Henry was a gifted ruler and administrator. He knew how to spot, and use, talented persons, and was more impressed by ability than by birth. The daily business of government was conducted by the officials of the Royal Household – the Justiciar (King's deputy), the Chancellor (King's secretary), the Chamberlain (Master of the Household) and, for military matters, the Marshal and the Constable. One reads of these great men being paid in

cash, bread, wine and candle ends! Most distinguished of all was the Justiciar Roger, Bishop of Salisbury, who sowed the seeds of modern administrative specialization by organizing the Court of Exchequer, appreciating the fact that effective government is founded on sound finance. The Royal judicial and fiscal policy was also furthered by the development of Itinerant Justices (Justices in Eyre) who made regular circuits during Henry's reign.

The peace which Henry gave England caused him to be deeply mourned when, in 1135, he died, leaving a vexed succession problem, which will shortly be explained.

The Gloucester Candlestick
(Victoria and Albert Museum. Crown Copyright)

Stephen, Great Seal, King's College, Cambridge
(By permission of the Provost & Fellows of King's College, Cambridge)

STEPHEN, 1135–1154

(Nephew of HENRY I, son of WILLIAM THE CONQUEROR'S daughter Adela, who married Stephen of Blois)

Born? 1097, was? 38 when he ascended the throne, and? 57 when he died.

Married Matilda, niece of HENRY I's first wife, and had two sons:

Eustace

William

The one-time Empress Matilda (see page 21), now married to Geoffrey of Anjou, should have become Queen. But she was out of England in 1135, and Stephen slipped in. There followed a chaotic reign, with intermittent Civil War.

Thumbnail Sketch   Mild, gallant, chivalrous and unfortunate.

WHAT TO REMEMBER

Henry I had suffered a personal and dynastic tragedy, when his only legitimate son, William, was drowned in the "White Ship" disaster of 1120. He had tried to offset this misfortune by persuading the barons to accept his daughter Matilda, widow of the Holy Roman Emperor and now wife of the Count of Anjou, as his heiress. The idea of a Queen regnant was, however, distasteful to the barons, who went back on their promise and accepted Stephen, son of the Conqueror's daughter Adela and her husband Stephen of Blois, as King. Stephen was fortunate in that he was the first claimant to arrive in England, fortunate also, at first, in the influence of his brother Henry of Blois, Bishop of Winchester, and in the support of the City of London, which had grown greatly in power during his uncle's reign.

But the choice was disastrous. Matilda, reputed to have "had the nature of a man in the frame of a woman", would not renounce her rights. Her uncle, David I of Scotland, stuck his oar into England's troubled waters, and was defeated at Northallerton (Battle of the Standard) in 1138. Her half-brother, Henry I's bastard son Robert of Gloucester, rose on her behalf; while some of the barons, notably the villainous tyrant of south-east England, Geoffrey de Mandeville, taking advantage of Stephen's weakness, made holiday in a welter of feudal anarchy, which was their happiest state. The grim words of the Anglo-Saxon chronicle have been frequently quoted: castles "filled with devils and evil men", exactions enforced by "unspeakable tortures", "Christ and his saints were asleep". Matilda herself landed in England in 1139, and Civil War swayed to and fro until 1148. Stephen was defeated and captured at Lincoln in 1141, London refused to accept Matilda as Queen, Stephen was released in exchange for Robert of Gloucester, Matilda escaped from Oxford Castle (1142) and fled over a snowbound country-side camouflaged in white. Darkness covered the land.

But, in 1152, Matilda having withdrawn to the continent four years previously, her son Henry appeared in England. Stephen's sons had, by now, died and, by the Treaty of Wallingford of 1153, it was arranged that this young Henry of Anjou should be his successor. Henry was not only master of Normandy, Maine, Anjou and Touraine, but had married, in 1152, Eleanor of Aquitaine, whose previous union with Louis VII of France had been dissolved. Thus, when Stephen died in 1154, he was followed by a sovereign whose continental dominions extended from the channel to the Pyrenees.

Adoration of the Magi, carved whalebone relief
(*Victoria and Albert Museum. Crown Copyright*)

Henry II, cast of effigy at Fontevrault
(Victoria and Albert Museum. Crown Copyright)

HENRY II, 1154–1189

(Son of Matilda and Geoffrey of Anjou – see pages 21 and 25 –
and grandson of HENRY I)

Born 1133, was 21 when he ascended the throne, and 56 when
he died.

Married Eleanor of Aquitaine, previously wife of Louis VII of
France (marriage dissolved). The unhappy marriage of Henry
and Eleanor produced eight children, five sons:

> William
> Henry
> Geoffrey
> RICHARD I
> JOHN

and three daughters. It also added to the domains of the English
crown the great duchy of Aquitaine, stretching from the Loire
to the Pyrenees.

Thumbnail Sketch Difficult in temperament, faithless in marriage –
an aristocratic leader who normally chose subordinates well. A
great contributor to the judicial and administrative systems of
England.

WHAT TO REMEMBER

Henry Plantagenet impressed his subjects by a powerful mind
trained in the continental fashion and by his vast possessions.
An anarchical England required a firm hand, and got it. Pacifica-
tion was swift, the development of "scutage" (shield money),
whereby the King took cash in lieu of military service, facilitated
the employment of mercenaries, whose professional mentality
was preferable to the circumscribed outlook of the feudal knight;
while the Assize of Arms of 1181, which prescribed the weapons
with which all men must provide themselves if called to serve,
was the germ of a militia.

For his first eight years Henry enjoyed the friendly assistance
of his brilliant Chancellor, Thomas à Becket. He judged ill,
however, in believing that with Becket as Archbishop of Canter-

bury (1162) it would be possible to solve the problem of Church and State. The two powers were at loggerheads over a number of subjects, of which the treatment of Clerks in Holy Orders accused of crimes was the most irritating. Clerks enjoyed "Benefit of Clergy", and could only be tried in Church Courts, where penalties were mild. Thus privileged were not only bishops, priests and deacons, together with the formidable monastic population, but also a host of subdeacons, acolytes, exorcists, readers and doorkeepers! Becket, graceful courtier metamorphosed into ascetic prelate, opposed Henry's solution, as laid down in the Constitutions of Clarendon (1164), that a clerk found guilty in the church courts should be unfrocked and passed to the royal justice for punishment. Thereupon he left for the continent, while the King controlled the vacant see and attempted to assure the future by having his son Henry crowned by the Archbishop of York at Westminster. The quarrel was patched up in 1170, Becket returned, disciplined those who had crowned the young Henry in his absence, provoked his King to a famous, hasty utterance, and was murdered in Canterbury Cathedral – thus achieving a triumph which was to last until the sixteenth century.

Events followed thick and fast. In 1170, also, Strongbow, Earl of Pembroke, started England's not uniformly happy connection

Font of Tournai Stone, Winchester Cathedral

with Ireland by crossing to that country and becoming King of Leinster, for which he did homage to Henry. In 1173–1174 there was rebellion on both sides of the channel in which Henry's wife and sons, William the Lion of Scotland and a number of barons were implicated. The King triumphed, his sons Henry and Geoffrey died, but his last years were poisoned by revolts on the part of Richard and the beloved John. The great man died unhappy in 1189.

He had established the Royal power as never before in England. The Assize of Clarendon (1166) developed Henry I's system of itinerant justices and concerned police measures necessary in a disorderly country (e.g. the criminal jury of presentment), while Possessory Assizes gave swifter satisfaction to persons who had been illegally dispossessed of land. Such measures started a legal system which would, eventually, be uniform throughout the country, one of the glories of England, the Common Law.

EARLY ENGLISH
1189–1307

Richard I (Coeur de Lion)	1189–1199
John (Lackland)	1199–1216
Henry III	1216–1272
Edward I	1272–1307

EARLY ENGLISH
Salisbury Cathedral, the Crossing

EARLY ENGLISH

1189–1307

"Early English" is the first of the three periods of architecture generally called "Gothic" – a derogatory term coined by Renaissance devotees of the classical tradition. Gothic differs from Norman above all by the use of the pointed arch. This device, obviously invented again and again in different places, solved the vital problem inherent in semicircular vaulting of how to build a stone roof over an oblong compartment without the awkwardness of having arches of varying heights: it thus assured the general use of stone rather than timber in roof construction, and thereby minimized the risk of fire by which so many wooden-roofed Norman churches had been destroyed.

The pointed arch, representing a tremendous structural advance, led to a lightness and elegance in building which could never be achieved in the Norman period. In the illustration "Salisbury Cathedral, the Crossing", note the pillars formed by clusters of shafts, note the grouped windows with their sharp "lancet" points, and note the small double windows with a hole punched above them, the forerunners of the "Geometrical Decorated" style.

Ornamentation, too, becomes increasingly sophisticated with the improved technique of craftsmen who employ the chisel rather than the axe – particularly noteworthy is the small, jutting "dog tooth" ornament which should be compared, but not confused, with the Norman zig-zag.

SOME 'EARLY ENGLISH' MOULDINGS

LINCOLN CATHEDRAL

PETERBOROUGH CATHEDRAL

BINHAM PRIORY, NORFOLK

Richard I, cast of effigy at Fontevrault
(Victoria and Albert Museum [on loan]. Crown Copyright)

RICHARD I (COEUR DE LION), 1189-1199

(Son of HENRY II and Eleanor of Aquitaine)

Born 1157, was 32 when he ascended the throne, and 41 when killed before Châlus.

Married Berengaria of Navarre, but had no children.

Thumbnail Sketch A handsome figure, an accomplished poet, a gifted soldier, an absentee ruler, a greedy, extravagant and cruel man.

WHAT TO REMEMBER

Richard I's coronation at Westminster was the first of these events to be fully documented, and did not differ essentially from the rite with which many of us are familiar today. But it introduced an unsatisfactory reign, for the new monarch was obsessed by a passion for soldiering, as such. For him there was little connection between war and policy,—"the glory that he sought was that of victory rather than conquest" (Stubbs). An attractive opportunity offered itself immediately in the Third Crusade, occasioned by the recapture of Jerusalem in 1187 by that distinguished Mahometan ruler, Saladin. So, in 1190, having raised the necessary cash by the sale of offices and charters, and by the release of William the Lion of Scotland from the fealty which he had sworn to Henry II, Richard set off for Palestine. The expedition, during which the Emperor Frederick Barbarossa was drowned and Richard quarrelled continually with Philip Augustus of France, achieved little except Saladin's promise that pilgrims might enter the Holy City. Richard started back in 1192, suffered shipwreck in the Adriatic and attempted to cross Germany in disguise. But Leopold, Duke of Austria, whom he had offended during the operations, apprehended him and handed him over to the Holy Roman Emperor, Henry VI. This highly romanticized episode (in the next century the French were to contribute the charmingly improbable story of Blondel twanging away beneath many a castle wall until answered by the royal captive) was, in reality, a matter of cash and politics. Henry demanded 150,000 marks, Philip Augustus and Richard's brother John intrigued to prolong the incarceration, but funds were produced and, in 1194, Richard reappeared in England for a few brief months.

However, the encroachments of Philip Augustus in Normandy, and the treachery of John, called Richard overseas once more, never to return. He forgave his brother and, during the remainder of his reign, engaged the French king in desultory campaigning, of which the splendid Château Gaillard stands as a memorial to this day. He met his death at the siege of Châlus, in pursuit of treasure, made the gesture of pardoning the archer who caused it – an example at once of chivalry and futility, for the man was subsequently executed with ingenious barbarity.

Credit for progress achieved in England during this reign must go to Hubert Walter, Archbishop of Canterbury and Justiciar during Richard's absence in France. The jury was further developed, responsibilities were given to the Knights of the Shire, foreshadowing the later system of Justices of the Peace, and more towns acquired charters.

The fact that he had Henry II as his father, and Hubert as his deputy, saved England in the reign of this picturesque absentee.

Balfour of Burleigh Ciborium
(Victoria and Albert Museum [on loan]. Crown Copyright)

John, effigy on his tomb in Worcester Cathedral

JOHN (LACKLAND), 1199–1216

(Son of HENRY II and Eleanor of Aquitaine, brother of
RICHARD I)

Born 1167, was 32 when he ascended the throne, and 48 when he
died.

Married Isabella of Gloucester (marriage dissolved), and, subsequently, Isabella of Angoulême. By his second marriage he had
five children, two sons:
> HENRY III
> Richard, Earl of Cornwall

and three daughters:
> > Joan – married Alexander II of Scotland
> > Isabella – married Emperor Frederick II
> > Eleanor – married first William the Marshal, Earl of
> > Pembroke, second Simon de Montfort, Earl of Leicester

Thumbnail Sketch   Selfish, vicious, cruel, tyrannical, violent in
love and hate, but capable – and a reader.

WHAT TO REMEMBER

John's behaviour as son and brother would not lead one to
view with optimism his accession as King, yet this reign had a
profound and not unsatisfactory influence upon English history.

It started with trouble abroad where Arthur of Brittany, son
of John's deceased elder brother Geoffrey, claimed Maine, Anjou
and Touraine, encouraged by his ally and overlord Philip
Augustus of France. The situation was aggravated by John's
marriage with Isabella of Angoulême, the betrothed of a certain
Count de la Marche, which gave Philip an excuse to take up arms
in vindication of that outraged nobleman. Major events in the
campaign were the capture by John, in 1203, of the seventeen
year-old Arthur, whose "dispiteous torture" and mysterious
death at Rouen has chilled the blood of Shakespearian audiences
since 1594, and the fall of Château Gaillard in 1204, betokening
the loss of Normandy. This event, like the abandonment of Calais
in 1558, was a blessing in disguise, stimulating a healthy and

necessary insularity, which was not affected by the retention of remoter Gascony.

War with Philip Augustus was followed by a breach with the formidable Pope Innocent III. When Hubert Walter died in 1205 two nominees were presented for the see of Canterbury, one by the Canterbury monks, the other by the King. Innocent set aside both these in favour of his own choice, the noble and intellectual Stephen Langton. Furious, John denied him entry and laid hands on church property. Innocent answered with the Interdict of 1208 – throughout England no bells, no public worship, no burial services, no sacraments, no ghostly comfort. John's excommunication followed in 1209, with its corollary – the sanctification of rebellion. Philip Augustus was happy to win merit by castigating this enemy of the Lord. John faced him, in alliance with the Emperor Otto IV, but, when threatened with invasion, made the astute *volte-face* of repentance and the presentation of England to Innocent as a papal fief. There followed, however, Philip Augustus' defeat of the Imperial and English forces at Bouvines in 1214, and John was left to face his barons, inspired by Stephen Langton.

The Great Charter, which they presented to him at Runnymede on 15 June 1215, is important because it expressed the belief that there were laws and customs in England which her kings must respect – even more important because in the seventeenth,

eighteenth and nineteenth centuries it was misinterpreted as the source from which British and American liberties flow.

Innocent III now supported his penitent by annulling Magna Carta, the barons sprang to arms, John led an army of mercenaries up and down the country, Louis, Dauphin of France, joined the insurgents and the unhappy King, depressed by the logistical disaster of having lost his baggage in the Wash, succumbed to dysentery at Newark in 1216.

Magna Carta

(By permission of the Trustees of the British Museum)

Henry III
Electrotype from the effigy by W. Torel
(By permission of the National Portrait Gallery)

HENRY III, 1216–1272

(Son of JOHN and Isabella of Angoulême)

Born 1207, was 9 when he ascended the throne, and 65 when he died.

Married Eleanor of Provence, and had two sons:
>EDWARD I
>Edmund, Earl of Lancaster

and three daughters:
>>Margaret – married Alexander III of Scotland
>>Beatrice
>>Katherine

Thumbnail Sketch   Religious, moral, artistic, cultivated, ambitious and ineffectual.

WHAT TO REMEMBER

A chaotic situation greeted the boy Henry III, yet in three years order was restored by William the Marshal, Gualo the Legate, and the Justiciar, Hubert de Burgh. Magna Carta was reissued, the Pope supported the King, the Dauphin Louis was defeated on land at the caricature battle of Lincoln, where there casualties were sustained, and at sea off Dover. He withdrew to France in 1217. On William the Marshal's death in 1219 Hubert de Burgh succeeded as Regent.

In 1227 Henry came of age, obsessed with ill-advised ambition to recover the lost French territories, despite Hubert's opposition. Encouraged by his tutor Peter des Roches, Bishop of Winchester, he blamed the Justiciar for the failure of a Poitou expedition in 1230, and dismissed him two years later.

Twenty-six years of personal misrule by Henry followed. Foreigners flooded the country – friends of Peter des Roches, attendants upon Henry's Queen, Italian nominees jostling for English benefices – to the indignation of the chronicler Matthew Paris, and despite the opposition of Grosseteste, Bishop of Lincoln. Immense contributions to the papal coffers and a foreign policy of peculiar ineptitude, aimed at the attainment of expensive luxuries – the Sicilian crown for Henry's son Edmund and

the Imperial diadem for his brother Richard – drained England
dry. Within our island itself Llewellyn ap Gruffydd defeated
Henry in Wales, thus crowning a record of failure which eventually roused the King's formidable brother-in-law Simon de
Montfort to take positive action against him.

Meeting in 1258, a council of barons headed by Simon forced
upon the King "The Provisions of Oxford", whereby future
government was to be controlled by a committee of fifteen. Henry
accepted this, in the first constitutional document to be published
in English, but got papal dispensation from his oath in 1259.
Nonetheless the baronial committee ruled England until 1261,
when Henry threw off its yoke. Fruitless negotiations deteriorated
into Civil War, whereupon both sides agreed to seek the arbitra-
tion of Louis IX of France. Saint Louis, famous for his judicial
decisions under the oak at Vincennes, believed firmly in royal
authority and freed Henry from the shackles of the Provisions by
the "Mise of Amiens" of 1264. War flared again and Simon
defeated Henry at Lewes, becoming, for a year, King of England
in all but name. In 1265 he assembled his famous Parliament in
London, calling up Knights from the shires and burgesses from
selected towns, but only twenty-three barons – evidence of his
increased reliance on the middle classes, for many magnates had
now gone over to Henry's side. The young Prince Edward
escaped from custody to unite these, and
Simon was defeated and killed at Evesham
on 4 August.

But Edward was a convert to de Montfort's
ideas, and the conception of the King being
under the law had now taken firm root.
The last seven years of the reign passed
quietly until, in 1272, Henry was buried in
Westminster Abbey, which he had loved and
rebuilt.

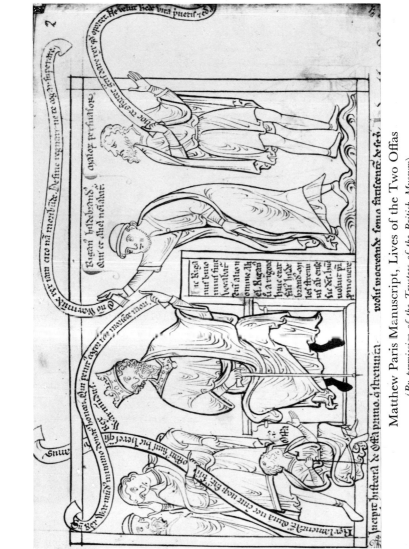

Matthew Paris Manuscript, Lives of the Two Offas

(By permission of the Trustees of the British Museum)

Edward I, Great Seal, King's College, Cambridge

(By permission of the Provost and Fellows of King's College, Cambridge)

EDWARD I, 1272–1307

(Son of HENRY III and Eleanor of Provence)

Born 1239, was 33 when he ascended the throne, and 68 when he died.

Married Eleanor of Castile, and had four sons:
>   EDWARD II (three died young)
and nine daughters.
Eleanor died at Harby in 1290 (crosses mark the places where her coffin rested: Northampton, Geddington, Waltham, Charing Cross)
Married Margaret of France, and had two sons:
>   Thomas of Brotherton, Earl of Norfolk
>   Edmund of Woodstock, Earl of Kent

Thumbnail Sketch Tall, handsome, a tough soldier, an athlete, honourable, strong, authoritative, effective – a commanding leader rather than a despot.

WHAT TO REMEMBER

The reign of this sensible King, who learnt from experience, has been described as a "period of definition" (Stubbs). The years 1275 to 1290 are rich in legislation, despite trouble at home and abroad between 1276 and 1307.

Accurate information should precede action, so Edward started by a countrywide investigation into the state of administration and justice. The first Statute of Gloucester (1278) enjoined itinerant justices to intensify enquiries by what right ("Quo Warranto?") certain privileges were exercised by great feudatories. The Statute of Mortmain (1279) stopped the transference of land into the "dead hand" of the Church, a practice which deprived the crown and other landowners of profitable feudal dues. The Statute of Acton Burnell (1283) protected merchants against their creditors, while the Statute of Winchester (1285) charged the common man with police duties, to the betterment of order within the realm. The second Statute of Westminster ("De Donis Conditionalibus" – 1285) encouraged the preservation of large estates by entail, thus making eldest sons the owners of broad acres and throwing cadets upon the world, which saved England from the closed caste of continental aristocracies. In 1290 the third Statute of Westminster ("Quia Emptores") allowed greater fluidity in land transactions whilst preserving the rights of feudal overlords.

Edward was also preoccupied with the Welsh, the Jews, the Scots and the French. Llewellyn ap Gruffyd was subdued in two systematic campaigns (1276–7 and 1282–3), being killed in the second, after which Wales was held down by the garrisons of great castles and flattered when the King's son, Edward, was made its Prince. In 1290 the King sought popularity and profit by expelling the Jews and made a bid to achieve the union of England and Scotland. The Scottish King, Alexander III, killed in a riding accident in 1286, was succeeded by his granddaughter, Margaret – "The Maid of Norway". It was agreed that she should marry Prince Edward, but she died in the Orkneys as she journeyed home. A succession dispute followed and Edward I, as arbitrator, chose John Balliol in 1292. He pestered his nominee with claims of overlordship until Balliol retaliated by forming with Philip IV of France, at war with Edward over Gascony, what would later be called "The Auld Alliance" (1295). Edward then sacked Berwick, deposed the defeated Balliol and brought the Coronation Stone from Scone to Westminster. War expenses dictated the summons of the "Model Parliament" (1295) which included seventy-four knights and two hundred and twenty

burgesses – the most comprehensive assembly which had met until then. But Scotland rose again under William Wallace, who, having overthrown an English army at Stirling Bridge, lost the battle of Falkirk to Edward in 1298, disappeared, but was eventually betrayed and executed in 1305. The mantle of Wallace fell on Robert Bruce, against whom Edward was preparing a major operation when death overtook him in July 1307.

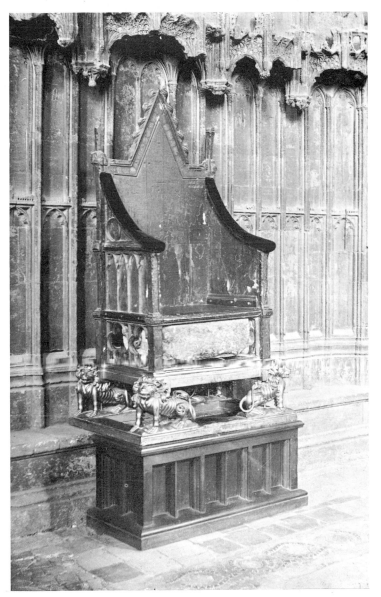

The Coronation Chair

(By courtesy of the Dean and Chapter of Westminster)

DECORATED

1307–1377

Edward II	1307–1327
Edward III	1327–1377

DECORATED
Exeter Cathedral, The Great West Window
(*By permission of the Dean and Chapter*)

DECORATED

1307–1377

"Decorated" is a bad title for an architectural period – there had been plenty of decoration before 1307, and much was to come thereafter – nevertheless, during the fourteenth century, building decreased in severity and gained in sumptuousness, despite Bannockburn (1314), the Hundred Years War (1337) and the Black Death (1348).

With glass easier to come by, our attention is particularly directed to windows where tracery first follows the circles and points of the geometrician but eventually throws off restraint and flows fantastically. The west window of Exeter Cathedral is a splendid example of geometrical tracery about to run riot, and the development from "the small double windows with a hole punched above them" of Early English Salisbury is obvious. (The hole has become the circle, the small double windows the tracery beneath.)

In addition to this, the eye is carried up by columns of increased height and delicacy, conventional foliage gives way to natural foliage in decoration, the ball flower ornament makes its appearance and the main ribs of vaults are connected up by little ones called "liernes".

SOME 'DECORATED' MOULDINGS

BALL-FLOWER   NATURAL FOLIAGE

KIDDINGTON, OXON, C. 1350   SOUTHWELL MINSTER, NOTTS, C. 1300

Edward II
From his effigy, sculptor unknown
(*By permission of the National Portrait Gallery*)

EDWARD II, 1307–1327

(Son of EDWARD I and Eleanor of Castile)

Born 1284, was 23 when he ascended the throne, and 43 when he died.

Married Isabella of France, and had two sons:
> EDWARD III
> John of Eltham, Earl of Cornwall

and two daughters:
>> Isabella
>> Joanna – married David II of Scotland

Thumbnail Sketch Strong and handsome in body, weak and foolish in character, "the first king after the conquest who was not a man of business" (Stubbs).

WHAT TO REMEMBER

Edward I left a difficult heritage of constitutional troubles, debt, and an unsolved Scottish problem. A powerful successor might have imposed an authoritarian régime, and Our Island's story would have been different, but the idle and incompetent Edward II was no professional – he found his pleasures in primitive agricultural pursuits, games, rowing, play-acting and the society of attractive young men.

One of these, the Gascon Piers Gaveston, exiled by Edward I, was now recalled and created Earl of Cornwall. The barons, whom he insulted with such humorous nicknames as "the fiddler", "whoreson" and "burst-belly", insisted on his rebanishment, but he unwisely returned. Cornered in Scarborough Castle, he was promised his life, but the Earl of Warwick, doubtless smarting under the sobriquet of "the black hound of Ardern", seized him, tried him illegally in the Great Hall of Warwick Castle and executed him on nearby Blacklow Hill (1312).

Real power in England lay, at this time, in the hands of a baronial committee of twenty-one Lords Ordainers (led by the King's first cousin, Thomas, Earl of Lancaster), who had drawn up certain Ordinances in 1311 which, like Magna Carta and the

Provisions of Oxford, limited the powers of the crown. In his humiliation Edward turned to new favourites – Hugh le Despenser (father) and Hugh le Despenser (son), the latter assuming the role previously played by Gaveston, though a man of far greater ability. Edward also attempted to offset domestic failure by the conquest of Scotland, a disastrous undertaking which disintegrated at Bannockburn (1314) when his army of 28,000 men fumbled its way to defeat by 10,000 determined opponents, skilfully led by Robert Bruce.

Lancaster, as inadequate a ruler as his monarch, failed to exploit this to his personal advantage, which led to the rise of a middle party of Barons, headed by the Earl of Pembroke – cold comfort for Edward, for its policy was to maintain the 1311 ordinances. Stresses and strains, however, destroyed the solidarity of baronial opposition, and Edward, with a flash of military energy, defeated the northerners at Boroughbridge (1322) and executed Lancaster at Pontefract.

Edward now ruled with the Despensers, whose administrative efficiency was counterbalanced by greed and ambition. The hated régime did not last long. Charles IV of France seized the greater part of Gascony in 1324. What more natural than that his sister, Edward's Queen Isabella, should visit him to negotiate, and that the young Prince Edward should follow to do homage for the duchy? These two were joined by Isabella's lover, the disaffected Marcher lord, Roger Mortimer, and a plot was hatched. There

was plenty of baronial support when the conspirators appeared in England, so they hanged the Despensers, imprisoned the King at Kenilworth and subsequently did him filthily to death in Berkeley Castle.

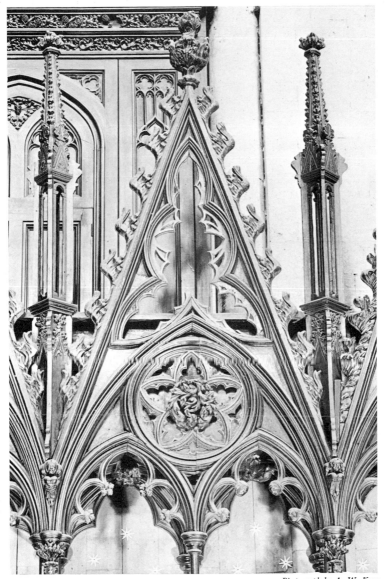

Photograph by A. W. Kerr

One of the canopies in the choir stalls, Winchester Cathedral

Edward III
Electrotype from the effigy in Westminster Abbey
(*By permission of the National Portrait Gallery*)

EDWARD III, 1327–1377

(Son of EDWARD II and Isabella of France)

Born 1312, was 14 when he ascended the throne, and 64 when he died.

Married Philippa of Hainault and had seven sons:
> Edward, the Black Prince
> Lionel of Antwerp, Duke of Clarence
> John of Gaunt, Duke of Lancaster
> Edmund of Langley, Duke of York
> Thomas of Woodstock, Duke of Gloucester
> (and two sons who died in infancy)

and five daughters, none of whom are important.

Thumbnail Sketch A vigorously attractive chivalrous character, greedy for glory, but no bad ruler – even if frivolous and extravagant in private life.

WHAT TO REMEMBER

During Edward III's inglorious minority Isabella and Mortimer acquiesced in a severe restriction of England's Gascon territory and recognised Scottish independence by the Treaty of Northampton (1328). Certain barons, apprehensive because of the execution of the King's uncle, the Earl of Kent, counselled Edward to assume the power, so Mortimer was hanged and Isabella withdrawn to luxurious life imprisonment (1330).

Edward was soon at war. Robert Bruce had died (1329) and Edward Balliol (John's son)· claimed the Scottish crown. An English army defeated Balliol's opponents at Halidon Hill (1333), but the young King, unable to impose his protégé upon Scotland, was soon preoccupied with greater events elsewhere.

Many reasons invited hostilities with France. The first Valois (Philip VI, 1328) harboured the Bruce faction and assisted them against Balliol, our Gascon possessions provided a perpetual irritant, and there was a wool trade crisis. England was then Europe's greatest wool producer, and, despite the arrival of the Fleming John Kempe at Norwich in 1331 and inducements offered to immigrant foreign weavers, most English wool was made into cloth in Flanders at Bruges, Ypres and Ghent. When Philip VI persuaded Louis of Flanders to arrest English merchants (1336), Edward stopped wool exports. On this the business-like Flemish burghers turned to England, while the Count of Flanders and his nobility sided with France; the Hundred Years War began.

This reign saw some twenty-one years of campaigning by highly trained professional English armies, greedy for loot and rape, but disciplined in action and equipped, militarily and socially, to overthrow the ponderous nonsense of French chivalry. The naval victory of Sluys (1340) cleared the seas, and Edward's claim of the French crown (as nephew to the sonless Charles IV) quietened the consciences of his Flemish allies, whose overlord was the King of France. (Incidentally, kings of England were to style themselves kings of France until 1801.) English bowmen inscribed the name of Crécy (1346) amongst our most distinguished battle honours, a subject for Rodin was provided by the burghers of Calais (an English town from 1347 to 1558), and the Black Prince won fame at Poitiers (1356). The Peace of Brétigny, though entailing renunciation of the French crown, brought Edward Aquitaine, Ponthieu and Calais, without feudal obligations, but, by 1375, the realistic operations of the modern-minded Du Guesclin had reduced our continental possessions to Calais, Cherbourg, Brest, Bordeaux and Bayonne.

Meanwhile at home the victory of Neville's Cross (1346) and the King's devastating foray to Edinburgh (1356) controlled the Scots. Successive Statutes of Labourers (1349 onwards) attempted to solve the social problems caused by the Black Death (1348-9), and English nationalism found further expression in anti-papal enactments (First Statute of Provisors 1351, First Statute of Praemunire 1353), whereby Papal patronage in England was restricted and appeals to Rome forbidden. In 1362 English became the language of the Law Courts, and there appeared William Langland's "Vision of Piers the Ploughman",

Wall painting, St. Stephen's Chapel, Westminster
(By permission of the Trustees of the British Museum)

written in the English tongue. Financial strain brought more frequent Parliaments, and Edward received collective petitions from his Commons, who now began to meet separately from the great magnates.

In 1377, predeceased by his Queen and by the Black Prince, with his rings torn from his fingers by his mistress Alice Perrers, Edward III died sadly and alone.

PERPENDICULAR
1377–1485

Richard II	1377–1399
Henry IV	1399–1413
Henry V	1413–1422
Henry VI	1422–1461
Edward IV	1461–1470
Henry VI (restored)	1470–1471
Edward IV	1471–1483
Edward V	1483
Richard III	1483–1485

PERPENDICULAR
Bath Abbey, The East Window
(*By permission of Pitkin Pictorials, Ltd*)

PERPENDICULAR

1377–1485

At this juncture, when continental architects whirl off into the extravagance and exuberance of the flamboyant, native austerity asserts itself and a style is developed which is peculiar to England.

Arches are flattened, windows are vast, walls display more glass than stone. Mullions run from bottom to top of these windows, right up to the arch – hence the name "Perpendicular" – and above it all we find frequently the glories of fan vaulting.

You could not have a better example of the style than in the accompanying view of the nave and east window of Bath Abbey. Note the piers, note the mullions and, in the roof, the fan vaulting.

SOME 'PERPENDICULAR MOULDINGS

ST. ALBANS, 1447

WELLS CATHEDRAL, 1465

HENRY VII CHAPEL,
WESTMINSTER, 1510

Richard II, artist unknown
(*By permission of the National Portrait Gallery*)

RICHARD II, 1377–1399

(Son of the Black Prince and Joan, Countess of Kent" the Fair
Maid of Kent". Grandson of EDWARD III)

Born 1366, was 11 when he ascended the throne, and 33 when
he died.

Married Anne of Bohemia, but had no children. Greatly affected
by her death in 1384. Subsequently married Isabella, daughter
of Charles VI of France. Marriage not consummated; she was
seven years old.

Thumbnail Sketch   A puzzle: courageous, luxurious (inventor of
the handkerchief!), foolish, immoderate in power, cheerful in
surrender – unstable.

WHAT TO REMEMBER

At the outset of this boy-king's reign power was exercised by
John of Gaunt together with Richard's mother and her coterie.
England, since a naval defeat off La Rochelle (1372), could not
defend herself against French raids, and flames flickered over
the Thames, Rye, Hastings, Lewes and the Isle of Wight.
National bellicosity was unimpaired, but heavy taxation paid
poor dividends and the contemporary establishment was
criticized bitterly. The Church, unpopular for its wealth and
discredited by the "Babylonish Captivity" of the Popes at
Avignon (1309–1378) and the "Great Schism" (1378–1415), was
under fire from the early reformer and eventual heretic John
Wycliffe, who translated the Bible into English, sent his itinerant
Lollards about the land and was fortunate only to suffer post-
humous burning.

England's smouldering discontent, springing from the Black
Death and dissatisfaction with serfdom and fixed wages, flared
up under the leadership of Wat Tyler, John Ball and Jack Straw,
in the Peasants' Revolt of 1381. Simon Sudbury, Archbishop of
Canterbury, and Sir Robert Hales, the Treasurer, were murdered,
and crisis point was reached when Wat Tyler fell in a scuffle
with the Mayor of London at Smithfield. Here the young King

took sole and courageous charge, promised redress and persuaded the rebels to disperse. Vested interests, however, prevailed and the disaffected counties were soon full of hangmen briskly plying their lugubrious trade.

Aged 17, Richard first attempted personal rule, assisted by his friend Robert de Vere, Earl of Oxford, with Michael de la Pole, Earl of Suffolk, as Chancellor. Soon, however, his uncle the Duke of Gloucester took control, after defeating an army led by Oxford at Radcot Bridge (1387). A group called the Lords Appellant – Gloucester, the Earls of Arundel and Warwick, Henry Bolingbroke, Earl of Derby (son of John of Gaunt, now absent in Spain), Thomas Mowbray, Earl of Nottingham – then used the Merciless Parliament (1388) to execute those of the King's friends whom they could apprehend, leaving Richard brooding on revenge, while his clerk of the works, one Geoffrey Chaucer, was busying himself more profitably with the Canterbury Tales.

In 1389 Richard seized power again and ruled sensibly for eight years. Stricken by the death of his first wife, Anne of Bohemia, but elated by an Irish progress in 1394 and peace with France in 1396, he took his vengeance in 1397. Gloucester was murdered and all the Lords Appellant were punished except Derby and Nottingham, who were promoted Dukes of Hereford and Norfolk. Their subsequent quarrel precipitated the scene in the lists at Coventry and banishment—six years for the former, life for the latter.

In 1399 John of Gaunt died. Hereford was his heir. Richard acted ruthlessly:

"... we seize into our hands
His plate, his goods, his money and his
lands,"

and disappeared to Ireland. In his absence the dispossessed Henry landed at Ravenspur and found plenty of support. Thereafter Richard surrendered lethargically in Wales, abdicated in London and was murdered at Pontefract.

Statue of the Virgin and Child, Winchester College

JOHN OF GAUNT AND HIS OFFSPRING

Crucial now is a clear picture of John of Gaunt and his offspring – this affects both HENRY IV and HENRY VII. Neither had an impeccable claim to the throne of England.

1. *The Succession of HENRY IV.*

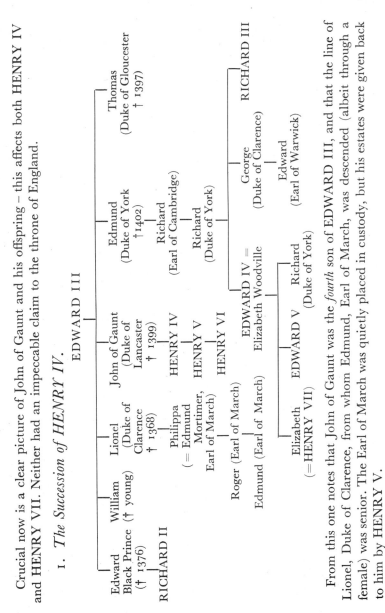

From this one notes that John of Gaunt was the *fourth* son of EDWARD III, and that the line of Lionel, Duke of Clarence, from whom Edmund, Earl of March, was descended (albeit through a female) was senior. The Earl of March was quietly placed in custody, but his estates were given back to him by HENRY V.

2. *The Succession of HENRY VII.*

The matrimonial arrangements of John of Gaunt were complicated. He was married three times:

(a) To Blanche of Lancaster (from whom he took the title of Lancaster). She died in 1369, having had three children, and her only son was HENRY IV.

(b) To Constance of Castile, by whom he had one daughter. She married back into Spain.

(c) To Catherine Swynford – daughter of Sir Payne Roet and widow of Sir Hugh Swynford. She had been his mistress for many years and her children – the Beauforts (the name comes from a French castle belonging to John of Gaunt) – were legitimised when he married her. It goes like this:

John of Gaunt = Catherine Swynford

- John Beaufort (Earl of Somerset)
- Henry Beaufort (Cardinal)
- Edmund Beaufort (Duke of Somerset)
- Thomas Beaufort (Duke of Exeter)
- Joan Beaufort = Earl of Westmorland
- Joan Beaufort = James I of Scotland

John Beaufort (Duke of Somerset)

Margaret Beaufort = Edmund Tudor, Earl of Richmond
(Edmund Tudor's father was Sir Owen Tudor, and his mother was Catherine of France, widow of Henry V)

HENRY VII = Elizabeth, daughter of Edward IV

So, in the veins of HENRY VII there ran the royal blood of England (watered down by illegitimacy) deriving from John of Gaunt. There was, also, the royal blood of France, deriving from his grandmother. There were other claimants, notably Edward Plantagenet, Earl of Warwick, descended in unimpeachable legitimacy, and exclusively through the male line, from Edmund, Duke of York (John of Gaunt's younger brother – see first family tree opposite). The first Tudor had good reason to be sensitive about his ancestry.

Henry IV, artist unknown
(*By permission of the National Portrait Gallery*)

HENRY IV, 1399–1413

(Son of John of Gaunt and Blanche of Lancaster, grandson of
EDWARD III and cousin of RICHARD II)

Born 1367, was 32 when he ascended the throne, and 46 when he
died.

Married Mary de Bohun, and had four sons and two daughters:

HENRY V	Blanche – married Louis
Thomas, Duke of Clarence	III, Elector Palatine of
John, Duke of Bedford	the Rhine
Humphrey, Duke of Gloucester	Philippa – married Eric
	XIII of Sweden

There were no children by his second marriage to Joanna of
Navarre.

Thumbnail Sketch A dour, businesslike politician.   Intelligent,
courageous and handsome; but not very attractive in character.
The first king to speak English as his native language.

WHAT TO REMEMBER

Henry Bolingbroke, Duke of Hereford and Duke of Lancaster,
now reigned as Henry IV. The note on page 72 "John of Gaunt
and his offspring" shows that the Earl of March had a superior
claim to the throne, thus Henry accepted his dependence upon
those whom Thomas Arundel, Archbishop of Canterbury, called
"the wise and ancient of his realm." But he was plagued by
rebellions.

The Earls of Huntingdon and Kent were the first trouble-
makers. They proposed to restore Richard II, but failed and
were executed, and Richard died mysteriously at Pontefract.
Then the attractive Owen Glendower, who had pursued legal
studies at Westminster, and was popularly thought to be assisted
by magic, rose in Wales. It took the rest of the reign to reduce
him, and he died a natural death in 1415. Meanwhile, in the
North, the great family of Percy became disaffected. They had
held the border country for some years, and had been good
friends to Henry. In 1402 Harry "Hotspur" (so he was called

by the Scots), son of the Earl of Northumberland, defeated and captured Archibald, Earl of Douglas, at Homildon Hill. The time had come, the Percys felt, for a royal reward. Dissatisfied with what the King offered, they and their prisoner now made common cause with Glendower and *his* prisoner, Sir Edmund Mortimer (Hotspur's brother-in-law and uncle to the Earl of March). The situation was saved by Henry's victory at Shrewsbury (1403), where Hotspur was killed, while the Earl of Northumberland suffered a short term of imprisonment. The old man was not quiet for long. In 1405 he conspired with Richard Scrope, Archbishop of York, and Thomas Mowbray, Earl of Nottingham (son of Henry's antagonist at Coventry). These two were captured and executed – this summary and successful punishment of an archbishop showing a change from the days of Becket – and Northumberland himself met his death at Bramham Moor in 1408.

Henry might show scant respect for the church in the person of Scrope, but he – and all men of property, ecclesiastical and lay – were merciless in their action against the Lollards, with their dangerously subversive condemnation of wealth. The statute "De Heretico Comburendo" (1401) sent many wretches to the stake, whilst the authorities of Oxford and Cambridge raised protective College walls to preserve the orthodoxy of their students.

In 1413 the King, wearied by quarrels with his ambitious heir, and suffering from diseases of the skin and the heart, fell into a fit while at his prayers in Westminster Abbey. He had long wished to go crusading, and died, not unsuitably, in the neighbouring Jerusalem Chamber on March 20.

Photograph by A. W. Kerr

A page of Winchester College Statutes, with the seal of
William of Wykeham (1400)

Henry V, artist unknown
(*By permission of the National Portrait Gallery*)

HENRY V, 1413–1422

(Son of HENRY IV and Mary de Bohun)

Born August 1387, was 25 when he ascended the throne, and 35 when he died.

Married Catherine of Valois, and had one son:
HENRY VI

Thumbnail Sketch   Brilliant general, conscientious administrator, typical example of medieval heroism and piety.

WHAT TO REMEMBER

Henry V, the most national of English kings up to this date, opened his reign with some sensibly conciliatory acts, such as the granting of liberty to the Earl of March, the restoration of Henry Percy (Hotspur's son) to his own, and the honourable interment of Richard II in Westminster Abbey. As "a true lover of the Holy Church", whose support he required, he pushed on the Lollard persecution, of which a distinguished victim was his erstwhile friend Sir John Oldcastle (Lord Cobham), who had planned an abortive rising against him.

He was, however, soon ready to "assume the port of Mars", knowing that glory abroad strengthens power at home. France, under a mad king (Charles VI) and harassed by the conflict of the Burgundian and Orleanist (Armagnac) parties, offered a tempting target. So Henry staked his claim to the French throne, dealt firmly with a conspiracy in which Richard, Earl of Cambridge, Lord Scrope of Masham and Sir Thomas Grey of Heton were involved, built a number of fine ships and crossed to Normandy with 10,000 men (1415). (Anecdotal historians rejoice in the financial aid given to Henry at this juncture by Richard Whittington, Lord Mayor of London for the third time in this reign). The successful siege of Harfleur (near Le Havre) cost him many casualties through dysentery, age-old scourge of armies in the field, and he decided to march to meet his fleet at Calais. A French feudal army, which vastly outnumbered Henry's, but which had forgotten the lessons taught by Du

Guesclin, lay across his road near Agincourt. 25 October 1415 was a day of glory, despite the ruthless slaughter of French prisoners, which has comforted later generations of Englishmen engaged in the Low Countries, and the King returned in triumph to London. A systematic and successful campaign in Normandy followed, the murder of their Duke by the Dauphin's adherents clamped the Burgundians firmly to the English side, and, by the Treaty of Troyes (1420), Henry became Regent and Heir of France, marrying into the bargain Catherine, the attractive daughter of Charles VI. The treaty did not mean the end of hostilities, for, while the victor bore off his bride to be crowned at home, his brother Thomas, Duke of Clarence, met defeat and death at Beaugé (1421). Back came the indefatigable Henry, on this occasion accompanied by his prisoner the 16 year-old James I of Scotland, retrieved the situation, and ended with a firm hold on Brittany, Normandy, Maine, Champagne and Guienne. But dysentery attacks commanders and private soldiers alike, and it was this disease which probably caused the King's death at Vincennes in August 1422. These brilliant conquests left an uneasy inheritance.

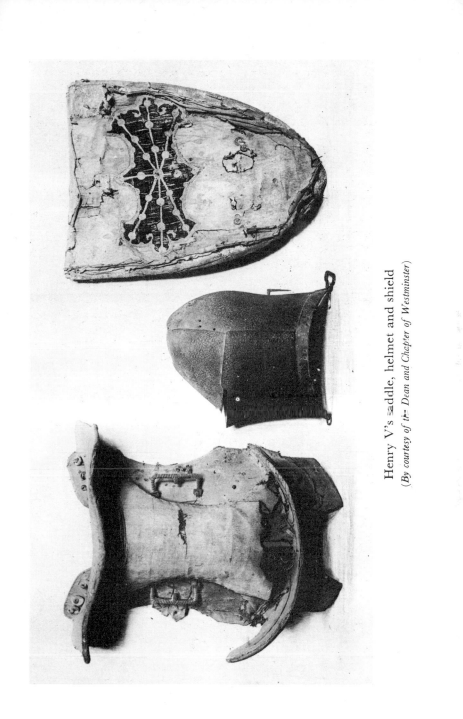

Henry V's saddle, helmet and shield

(By courtesy of the Dean and Chapter of Westminster)

Henry VI, artist unknown
(*By permission of the National Portrait Gallery*)

HENRY VI, 1422–1461

(Son of HENRY V and Catherine of Valois)

Born 1421, was nearly 1 when he ascended the throne, and nearly 50 when he died.

Married Margaret of Anjou, and had one son:
Edward, Prince of Wales

Thumbnail Sketch   Virtuous, religious, scholarly – but no ruler for a troubled age.

WHAT TO REMEMBER

The infant Henry VI succeeded to the English throne on 31 August 1422 and, technically, to that of France on the death of Charles VI a few weeks later. His uncles functioned as Regents – Humphrey, Duke of Gloucester (generous donor of books to Oxford) in England, and John, Duke of Bedford, in France.

In France the Dauphin, ironically styled "The King of Bourges", ruled the territory south of the Loire, less Gascony. To this inept young man there came, in 1429, Joan of Arc, who carried him through victories at Orléans and Patay to coronation at Rheims. Next year the Maid was captured by the Burgundians and sold to the English, to be burnt at Rouen in 1431. Her revitalization of France, together with the death of Bedford (1435) and Burgundy's abandonment of the English alliance, shattered our continental Empire. By 1453 everything was lost except Calais. The Hundred Years War was over.

At home jealousies and stresses marked the King's minority. Gloucester quarrelled with the Beauforts (see note page 73) and their friend, William de la Pole, Earl of Suffolk. The latter negotiated Henry's marriage with the enchanting but formidable Margaret of Anjou – agreeing, in a secret clause, to the surrender of Anjou and Maine. With her support, and that of Edmund Beaufort, Duke of Somerset, he accused Gloucester of treason before a parliament at Bury St. Edmunds (1447) shortly after which "Good Duke Humphrey" died mysteriously. Disaster in France exacerbated the situation at home, and men remembered that their King – now subject to sporadic madness – was descended from a usurper. Suffolk, the scapegoat, was banished for five years, but Henry's authority did not extend to the channel – the earl was arrested and executed at sea. In 1450 discontent at governmental incompetence brought Jack Cade's abortive insurrection, followed by an intensification of rivalry between Somerset and Richard, Duke of York. York proved an able Protector during Henry's incapacitation by insanity (1453–4) but Somerset, after a spell in the Tower, returned to power when the King recovered. This drove York to fight, and the Wars of the Roses (1455–1485) began. Ordinary folk were little affected, but the great played power politics and, with their retainers (mostly old soldiers home from France) tramped England fighting dreary battles, the names of which awaken faint echoes in the traveller's mind without any quality to stir the soul. Somerset fell at St. Albans in 1455, York at Wakefield in 1460, but the latter's son, Edward, prevailed at Towton in 1461 and was crowned at Westminster, while Henry and Margaret fled to Scotland.

Thus ended, effectively, the reign of Henry VI. He left to England, which he could not rule, two bright jewels: Eton and King's College, Cambridge (modelled on William of Wykeham's foundations of Winchester and New College, Oxford), witnesses to his real love of godliness and learning.

Tomb of Archbishop Chichele, Canterbury Cathedral (1443)

Edward IV, artist unknown
(*Reproduced by Gracious Permission of Her Majesty The Queen*)

EDWARD IV, 1461–1483

(Son of Richard, Duke of York, and Cicely Neville,
great-great-grandson
of EDWARD III, as was HENRY VI)

Born 1442, was 19 when he ascended the throne, and 40 when he died.

Married Elizabeth Woodville, and had two sons:
> EDWARD V
> Richard of York

and five daughters. HENRY VII was to marry Elizabeth, the eldest.

Thumbnail Sketch Cultivated, sensual, genial, commercial with a streak of ruthlessness.

WHAT TO REMEMBER

The big man at the start of the reign of Edward IV was the King's cousin, Richard Neville. He inherited the Earldom of Salisbury, gained that of Warwick by marrying Anne Beauchamp, its heiress, sought popularity by picturesque hospitality, and earned the sobriquet "Warwick the Kingmaker". Kingmaker and King, however, were not long left in peace by the indefatigable Margaret of Anjou, but her adherents were defeated at Hexham (1464) and, in the following year, Henry VI was apprehended and lodged in the Tower.

Meanwhile Edward, who was finding the Neville influence irksome, wooed and secretly wed a Lancastrian widow, one Elizabeth Gray (née Woodville), when Warwick would have preferred a dynastic union with a European royalty. It was also Warwick's policy to seek a French alliance, a hope shattered when Edward arranged to marry his sister Margaret with Charles the Bold of Burgundy (1468). Then came a shower of new peerages and glittering matches for the Woodvilles, and Warwick turned to his son-in-law, George, Duke of Clarence, the King's brother.

The exchanges of the next three years were rapid and bloody.

Warwick and Clarence rose in insurrection, incarcerated the King at Middleham, slaughtered a number of Woodvilles and then released their apparently chastened royal captive. Edward rounded on them in 1470 and harried them out of the land. At the court of Louis XI Warwick made the *volte-face* of reconciliation with Margaret of Anjou, and betrothed his younger daughter to the Prince of Wales, Margaret's son. Now Warwick and Clarence landed at Dartmouth, Edward IV sought asylum with Charles the Bold, while Henry VI was brought out of the Tower for a short restoration. Early in 1471 Edward reappeared at Ravenspur, was joined by the self-seeking Clarence, defeated and killed Warwick at Barnet, beat Margaret (killing the Prince of Wales) at Tewkesbury and sent his brother Richard, Duke of Gloucester, on a mission to the Tower of London, whereupon Henry VI, reincarcerated there, conveniently died.

The remaining years of the reign saw Edward ruling prosperously and autocratically. The normal income of the crown was swollen by the sequestered estates of nobles condemned for treason, by customs dues (there were vast profits from wool), by amiable business relations with London bankers and merchants (was not Edward's genial mistress Jane Shore the wife of a goldsmith?) and by benevolences (forced loans). An expedition to France (1475) led to a realistic agreement with Louis XI, who

at the Treaty of Pecquigny, thought it worthwhile to present Edward with 75,000 crowns, followed by an annual pension of 50,000. And there was a pleasant friendship with William Caxton, who first printed in England in 1476, and, finally, the comfort of getting rid of "false, fleeting, perjured Clarence" in 1478. Imprisoned for treason, this unreliable Duke did not long survive in the Tower – though whether or not he was "wash'd to death with fulsome wine" in the famous Malmsey butt, no one will ever know. Edward, himself, died suddenly in 1483.

Photograph by A. W. Kerr

Wall paintings, Eton College Chapel (c. 1479)

Edward V

Illustrated MS. of Dictes and Sayings, Library of
Lambeth Palace

EDWARD V, 1483

(Son of EDWARD IV and Elizabeth Woodville)

Born 1470, he ascended the throne, and died, at the age of 12.

Thumbnail Sketch With his younger brother, Richard of York, one of the "Princes in the Tower". It is impossible to sketch the character of this child.

WHAT TO REMEMBER

This tragic "reign" lasted for less than three months. Shortly after the death of Edward IV, Edward V's uncle, Lord Rivers, and half-brother, Sir Richard Gray, started on their fateful progress with the twelve-year-old King from Ludlow to London. Another of Edward's uncles, Richard, Duke of Gloucester, accompanied by the Duke of Buckingham, intercepted the party en route. Rivers and Gray were hustled off to prison and subsequent death at Pontefract, and the weeping child continued his way to London, and the forbidding hospitality of the Tower, in Richard's care. Meanwhile the Queen, together with her daughters and the small Duke of York, had sought sanctuary in Westminster Abbey.

Gloucester had been named Protector, and consolidated his position by the ruthless and summary execution of Lord Hastings, who opposed him on the Council. His next step was to wheedle Richard of York out of the care of his mother and the Church, and to lodge him with his brother in the Tower. A Dr. Ralph Shaw was put up to preach a propaganda sermon at St. Paul's Cross wherein he alleged that the little Princes were illegitimate, on the assumption that Edward IV had broken his betrothal to Eleanor Butler in order to marry Elizabeth Woodville. After a number of modest refusals Richard eventually accepted Buckingham's suggestion that he was the rightful heir, and proceeded to his coronation on 6 July 1483.

And what of the two princes? In *The Times* of 20 March 1963 Dr G. R. Elton wrote as follows: "Whether Richard III killed the princes may well have to remain an unsettled question, though anyone who has ever looked at the evidence with care will have to agree that in all probability they were dead before the end of his reign. They may have been disposed of on somebody else's orders; they might even have died a natural death, as two children harshly treated in the fifteenth century Tower were only too likely to. What is certain is that Richard usurped the crown, on a transparent pretext, accusing his nephews of a bastardy which even 'the good duke's' defenders do not credit. Experience had proved how dangerous a royal minority could be to the dynasty and the nation, and no doubt Richard's action, while certainly ambitious, was also politically sensible in its crude way. In other words, he was a competent and hard-bitten politician of the kind likely to be successful in his day . . . ."

Let Shakespeare, biased Tudor propagandist or not, have the last word:

"Dream on thy cousins smother'd in the Tower:
Let us be lead within thy bosom, Richard,
And weigh thee down to ruin, shame, and death!
Thy nephews' souls bid thee despair, and die!"

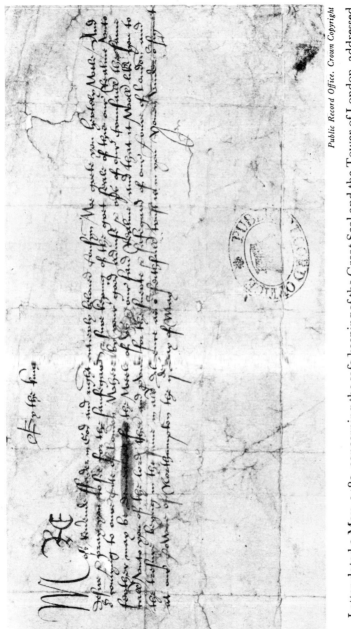

Letter dated 2 May, 1483, concerning the safe-keeping of the Great Seal and the Tower of London, addressed to Thomas Bourchier, Cardinal Archbishop of Canterbury, and bearing the signature of Edward V

Richard III, artist unknown
(*By permission of the National Portrait Gallery*)

RICHARD III, 1483–1485

(Son of Richard, Duke of York, and Cicely Neville,
great-great-grandson of

EDWARD III, brother of EDWARD IV, uncle of EDWARD V)

Born 1452, was 30 when he ascended the throne, and 32 when
he died.

Married Anne Neville (daughter of Warwick the Kingmaker)
and had one son, who died aged 10.

Thumbnail Sketch   Fine commander and administrator, but
ruthlessly ambitious.

WHAT TO REMEMBER

It was not possible for the new King to disguise the ruthlessness
of his usurpation of the throne, indeed "among the curious
obsessions with history, the endeavour to 'rehabilitate' Richard
III must rank second only to the Baconian heresy" (Dr G. R.
Elton. *ibid.*). The report that the little princes had died shocked
public opinion, and Buckingham, ruminating perhaps on the
dangers to which his own adhuivinve of royal blood might expose
him, dropped the role of supporter for that of conspirator. In
October 1483 he led an insurrection with which everything went
wrong, and which brought him to the block at Salisbury. Henry
Tudor, Earl of Richmond (see note page 73 on the Succession of
Henry VII) had sailed from Brittany as part of this plan, but
prudently withdrew from Plymouth in view of the unpromising
intelligence which he gathered there. Richard, meanwhile,
sought popularity by every means in his power, of which the
calling of a parliament, in 1484, which forbad the levying of
benevolences, was one. His dynastic position deteriorated with
the death of his son Edward, Prince of Wales, at Middleham in
the April of that year and men's thoughts turned increasingly
to the Earl of Richmond. In March 1485 the Queen, "that
wretched Anne", followed her son to the grave, though there is
no evidence to prove that her end was hastened by her husband,
however advantageous the match which he contemplated with

the Princess Elizabeth, Edward IV's eldest daughter, might have been.

But across the Channel, at Harfleur, discontented Englishmen were gathering, French soldiery were being recruited and "princely Richmond" was fitting out a second expedition. On 1 August he sailed and, seven days later, knelt in prayer at Milford Haven. Under the emblems of St. George of England and the Red Dragon of Wales he advanced, met and killed Richard at the decisive battle of Bosworth Field. "Here, indeed, was one of fortune's freaks: on a bare Leicestershire upland, a few thousand men in close conflict foot to foot, while a few thousand more stood aside to watch the issue, sufficed to set upon the throne of England the greatest of all her royal lines, that should guide her through a century of change down new and larger streams of destiny, undreamt of by any man who plied bow and bill that day in the old-world quarrel of York and Lancaster." (G. M. Trevelyan. History of England.)

Visored Sallet
(*Victoria and Albert Museum. Crown Copyright*)

TUDOR

1485–1558

Henry VII	1485–1509
Henry VIII	1509–1547
Edward VI	1547–1553
Mary	1553–1558

TUDOR

Compton Wynyates, Tysoe, Warwick

TUDOR

1485–1558

One would hardly expect the period which saw the breach with Rome and the Dissolution of the Monasteries to be prolific in churches, though Westminster Abbey was enriched by the magnificence of Henry VII's Chapel. This was a time when prices were rising, when quick money was being made and when successful merchants turned themselves rapidly into landed proprietors, as is the way with Englishmen. Up and down England, in town and country, houses arose deriving from the Perpendicular style of architecture and with a hint or two of the fortifications of earlier days. There was much use of brick, there was half-timbered work, there was stone – in fact houses varied from district to district according to the availability of materials. Look at Compton Wynyates – a perpendicular arch, mullioned windows, old style machicolation and new style chimney stacks, brick, stone and half-timber. Here is the essence of the Tudor period.

Anno ḣ o ṡ ẓo octob᷎ ṃago ḣenẓick vıı tᵃᵘ᷎᷍ᵗ᷍ eᵗgᵉ ıllⁱſtᵒſſⁱma
oᵗᵈⁱⁿata ꝑ ᵈᵉᵐᵉⁱⁿ zⁱⁿık ꝶ᷎ ᵗᵉgⁱᵉ ṃᵉ ᷎ᵛⁱſſⁱᵒⁱᵒ᷍ ·

Henry VII, attributed to Michel Sitium (1505)
(*By permission of the National Portrait Gallery*)

HENRY VII, 1485–1509

(Son of Margaret Beaufort and Edmund Tudor, Earl of Richmond, great-great-grandson of John of Gaunt, great-great-great-
grandson of EDWARD III – see note on "John of Gaunt and
his offspring", page 72).

Born 1457, was 28 when he ascended the throne, and 52 when he
died.

Married Elizabeth of York, daughter of EDWARD IV, and had
two sons:
>Arthur, Prince of Wales
>HENRY VIII,

and two daughters:
>Margaret (married James IV of Scotland) and
>Mary (married (1) Louis XII of France, (2) Duke of
>Suffolk)

Thumbnail Sketch A clear-headed politician, a transitional
character from the Middle Ages to the Renaissance.

WHAT TO REMEMBER

A boss in Winchester Cathedral depicts a crown upon an
improbable shrub, reminding us that the crown of England was
found in a hawthorn bush at Bosworth. This crown, bandied
about during thirty troubled years, was firm upon the King's head
when Henry VII died.

Henry had a hard task. A number of persons had better right
to the throne than he, but he eliminated the young Earl of Warwick (whose claim was transmitted exclusively through the male
line), first by imprisonment, then by execution, and married
another potential trouble maker – Elizabeth, daughter of Edward
IV. Nevertheless he suffered irritating impersonations by Lam-
bert Simnel, a baker's son, and Perkin Warbeck, a Netherlands
Jew. Simnel pretended to be Warwick and, after his defeat at
Stoke (1487), was suitably employed in the royal kitchens.
Warbeck, masquerading as the younger of the "Princes in the
Tower", was hanged. Overmighty subjects who, with bands of
retainers, had ravaged England during the Wars of the Roses,

were restrained by the Statute of Livery and Maintenance and supplanted on the King's Council by members of the lesser nobility and middle class. The Council, governing through squirearchical Justices of the Peace, and functioning judicially by means of its sub-committee the Star Chamber, and other prerogative courts, reinforced normal justice and revived the respect for law which the nation had lost.

"Money makes the man"; how much more does it make the king. Economy was practised, royal estates yielded profits, feudal privileges were exploited and ingenious exactions were conceived by hard-headed ecclesiastics like Morton and Fox, and those "ravening wolves" Empson and Dudley. Overseas trade was stimulated and particularly favourable treaties were made with the Flemings, who badly needed English wool for their cloth industry.

Foreign policy, also, was made to pay by playing off France and Spain against each other. The Treaty of Medina del Campo (1489) bound us to the latter, a cautious expeditionary force landed on the continent and was bought off by the former (Treaty of Etaples, 1492). In 1501 Henry's elder son, Arthur, was married to Catherine of Aragon and, in 1502, his daughter, Margaret, to James IV of Scotland – to cut a dash on the European stage and secure the northern flank. Meanwhile John Cabot had sailed to America under Henry's patronage (1497), and

Erasmus had crossed the channel to converse with Grocyn, Lily, Linacre and Colet and make the agreeable discovery that "when you go anywhere on a visit the girls all kiss you".

By 1509 the crown was secure, the coffers were full, governmental machinery functioned and England was respected abroad.

Photograph by Chaplin Jones

Roof boss showing Prince of Wales feathers (remember Tudor emphasis on Wales) in the church of St. Peter and St. Paul, Godalming.

En expressa vides Henrici Regis imago
Qva fvit octavi mvsis hoc strvxit asylvm
Magnifice cvm ter denos regnasset et ono
Annos: qvis maior regem labor vltimvs ornet

Henry VIII, by Hans Eworth after Holbein
(*By courtesy of the Master and Fellows of Trinity College, Cambridge*)

HENRY VIII, 1509–1547

(Son of HENRY VII and Elizabeth of York)

Born 1491, was 17 when he ascended the throne, and 55 when he died.

Married Catherine of Aragon (1509) – daughter MARY
      Anne Boleyn (1533)   – daughter ELIZABETH I
      Jane Seymour (1536)   – son EDWARD VI
      Anne of Cleves (1540)
      Catherine Howard (1540)
      Catherine Parr (1543)

Thumbnail Sketch Renaissance scholar and athlete, new world autocrat, possessed Tudor gift of handling Englishmen.

WHAT TO REMEMBER

Henry VIII inherited a firm throne and a full treasury. England rejoiced in "youth like summer morn", a delight increased by his marriage, with papal dispensation, to his brother Arthur's widow, the popular Catherine of Aragon, and also by the execution of Empson and Dudley, the first of Henry's many acts of political opportunism.

A short involvement in continental war (the main event at home being the defeat of James IV of Scotland at Flodden, 1513) threw up Thomas Wolsey, brilliant planner and administrator, Archbishop of York in 1514 and, in 1515, Chancellor.

For a time Wolsey exercised his diplomatic genius in attempting to achieve balance of power in Europe between Francis I of France and the Holy Roman Emperor Charles V. The game was played at the Field of Cloth of Gold (1520) with Francis, and at less sumptuous but more realistic meetings with Charles. Francis' defeat by Charles at Pavia (1525) upset this balance, and Charles' capture of Rome (1527) affected Henry deeply.

The dynasty needed a male heir and the marriage with Catherine had produced a daughter, Mary, and a melancholy tale of miscarriages and children still-born or dying in infancy. Henry probably sensed divine displeasure (had he not married his brother's widow?) and he required divorce. Catherine was the

Emperor's aunt – it was unlikely that the Pope would help Henry, with Rome in the hands of Catherine's nephew. Nor could Wolsey arrange matters satisfactorily, so Wolsey was dismissed and fortunately died before facing trial for High Treason (1530).

Abroad a wind of change was blowing. Luther had nailed his theses to the Wittenberg church door in 1517, Zwingli had denounced various catholic tenets at Zurich, and Calvin, not yet established at Geneva, had preached "a purer devotion" at Bourges. There was no certainty that these ideas would capture England, but the Church here was unpopular because of its wealth, because of Renaissance ideas, and because of the suspicion which nationalism entertains for an international institution. There followed a momentous period when Henry exploited this unpopularity to his own advantage. Using the "Reformation Parliament" (1529–1536) he progressed to the position of "Supreme Head of the Church of England" (Act of Supremacy, 1534), and Thomas More and Fisher, Bishop of Rochester, were executed for refusing to accept this. Meanwhile Archbishop Cranmer, having taken advice of European universities, pronounced the marriage with Catherine invalid, and Henry embarked upon a tedious series of matrimonial adventures. With Thomas Cromwell as his Vicar-General, relics and shrines were destroyed (1538), the monasteries were dissolved (1536, 1539)

The Great Harry, by R. Cruickshank
(*By courtesy of the Trustees, National Maritime Museum*)

with little opposition except Robert Aske's "Pilgrimage of Grace" (1536). The doctrinal pendulum swung between concessions to protestantism and attempts to safeguard the old faith (Cranmer's Bible in English and the Six Articles, 1539). Henry's ideal was non-papal catholicism, but "to all men alike the state was their real religion and the King their great High Priest" (Pollard).

The closing years brought war. James V of Scotland, a papal supporter, sent an army to disgraceful defeat at Solway Moss (1542) and died, brokenhearted, leaving the infant Mary Stuart as heiress. Henry, wishing to marry his son Edward to this child, pursued a rough wooing by sacking Edinburgh, and declared war on France to prevent a Franco-Scottish match. Peace came in 1546 and, next year, the wreck of Henry VIII, scholar, musician, Defender of the Faith, power politician, founder of our permanent navy – a monarch in the grand manner – died.

Edward VI, after Holbein
(*By permission of the National Portrait Gallery*)

EDWARD VI, 1547–1553

(Son of HENRY VIII and Jane Seymour)

Born 1537, was 9 when he ascended the throne, and 15 when he died.

Thumbnail Sketch A cold child of advanced and cultivated intelligence.

WHAT TO REMEMBER

This reign was dominated by the Duke of Somerset (1547–1549) and then by the Duke of Northumberland (1549–1553).

The Council of Regency, appointed by Henry VIII to rule England during Edward's minority, allowed Edward Seymour, Earl of Hertford, later Duke of Somerset (Jane Seymour's brother) the office of Protector. Somerset combined democratic idealism, tolerance, avarice and self-satisfaction with a dangerous ignorance of practical politics. He, like the late King, appreciated the possibility of uniting England and Scotland by marrying Edward with the infant Mary, Queen of Scots, but "the manner of the wooing" (invasion, the defeat of the Scots at Pinkie, the sack of Edinburgh again in 1547) remained unfortunate, and the Scottish regent Arran despatched Mary to France to wed the unattractive prince who later became Francis II. Somerset's religious policy of moderate protestantism meant the repeal of heresy laws and other relaxations of Henry VIII's non-papal catholicism, leading to an influx of continental reformers. The Dissolution of the Chantries (1547) – logical, if masses for the dead are deemed superstitious – stopped the educational ministrations of the chantry priests, "schools are not maintained", wrote Latimer, and the "King Edward VI Grammar Schools" were totally inadequate to offset this loss. Cranmer's masterly middle-way Prayer Book of 1549 (enforced by an Act of Uniformity) aroused considerable opposition, particularly from Cornishmen who knew the Mass but regarded English as a foreign tongue. In addition prices had doubled since the beginning of the century in England, as everywhere else in Europe, and there was unemployment in the countryside, largely caused by enclosures for sheep farming, whereby hard-headed *parvenu* landlords got rich quickly. Agrarian revolts followed, notably that of Robert Ket in Norfolk (1549), ruthlessly suppressed by John Dudley, Earl of Warwick (later Duke of Northumberland). These disturbances provided the opportunity which this go-getter required: Somerset had failed, and the Council lodged him in the Tower.

Northumberland was now the most influential man in England. Inheriting the unscrupulous qualities of his father, Henry VII's "ravening wolf" Edmund Dudley, he thought solely of money and power. He sought popularity by supporting the extreme protestants and the profiteer landlords, and financial gain by the spoliation of churches and guilds and the exploitation of the peasantry. The 1549 Prayer Book was replaced by the much more protestant work of 1552, accompanied by a new Act of Uniformity. "Somerset had his head cut off", the King noted unfeelingly in his journal, but he was soon to follow his uncle. In 1552 he had measles and smallpox, 1553 brought a galloping consumption. Northumberland, panic-stricken at the prospect of the succession of the catholic Mary Tudor, sponsored an alternative and unwilling claimant in his daughter-in-law, Lady Jane Grey (great-granddaughter of Henry VII), to whom Edward was persuaded to leave the throne by will. The King died, Northumberland found himself deserted by the Council, and so staked all on the desperate *volte-face* of proclaiming Mary queen and sacrificing Lady Jane.

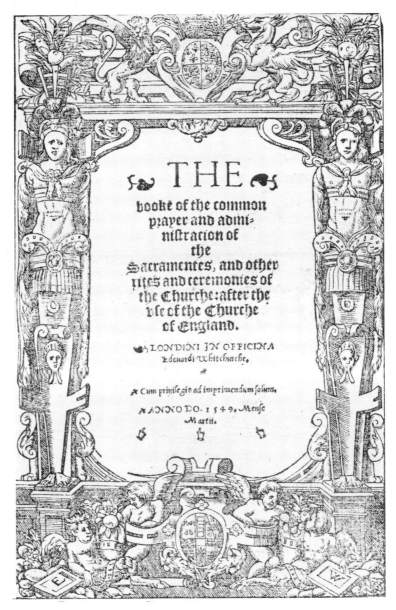

Book of Common Prayer (1549)
(By permission of the Trustees of the British Museum)

Mary, artist unknown
(*By permission of the Master and Fellows of Trinity College, Cambridge*)

MARY, 1553-1558

(Daughter of HENRY VIII and Catherine of Aragon and half-sister of EDWARD VI)

Born 1516, was 37 when she ascended the throne, and 42 when she died.

Married Philip II of Spain, but had no children.

Thumbnail Sketch   Highly educated, deeply religious and, despite the sobriquet "Bloody Mary", probably the most merciful of the Tudors.

WHAT TO REMEMBER

The accession of Mary, whose mother, Catherine of Aragon, had always inspired sympathy and affection, was welcomed with optimistic junketing. Northumberland had gone too far in his championship of advanced protestantism, and in the blatant egotism of the Lady Jane Grey plot. Many Englishmen would now have accepted a return to the Church as it had been under Henry VIII, and the majority found no tears to shed when the unprincipled Duke was executed.

Mary was quick to dismiss the more prominent protestant bishops from their sees, and Parliament, meeting in October 1553, repealed the religious legislation of the previous reign. So far, so good – but when it became clear that the Queen had set her heart on marrying Philip of Spain, there was opposition from Englishmen who feared loss of national independence, and who dreaded the Inquisition. A rebellion, of which Sir Thomas Wyatt was the leader, took place early in 1554, and brought him to the block, together with Lady Jane Grey and her husband, Lord Guildford Dudley, Northumberland's son. Meanwhile Mary's half-sister Elizabeth was put under restraint, first in the Tower and subsequently at Woodstock.

In July 1554 Philip and Mary were married, with the rites of the old church, in Winchester Cathedral, and in November the Papal legate, Cardinal Pole, absolved the country, in Parliament, from the sin of schism. Coming events cast their shadows before them in the revival of the anti-Lollard statute of 1401 about the burning of heretics – "De Heretico Comburendo" – and all acts passed against Rome since 1528 were swept away. Parliament, however, made it abundantly clear to the Queen that the mighty vested interest represented by the confiscated land and property which had once belonged to the monasteries, the chantries and the guilds must be left undisturbed.

In 1555 the notorious Marian persecution began – the accounts of which, in Foxe's Book of Martyrs, were to make the blood of protestant Englishmen run cold for many generations. The courage of men like Cranmer, Latimer and Ridley did, indeed, "light a candle" and achieved the ruin of the cause upon which the Queen had set her heart. Yet, when contrasted with continental holocausts, England's sufferings seem mild, and it is to be remembered that Mary, though stern with the heretic, was comparatively lenient with the traitor.

The reign ended with an anomalous situation whereby England supported Spain in war against France (1557), anomalous because Pope Paul IV, who wished to drive the Spaniards from Italy, figured amongst this catholic Queen's enemies. Calais was lost in January 1558, and Mary died in the following November amidst rejoicings as heartfelt as those which had greeted her when she came to the throne.

Jug cased in pierced silver gilt
(*Victoria and Albert Museum. Crown Copyright*)

ELIZABETHAN

1558–1603

Elizabeth I   1558–1603

ELIZABETHAN
Longleat, Wiltshire

ELIZABETHAN

1558–1603

During this exuberant reign social problems abounded, but it was still possible to get rich quickly. The *parvenus* of the period had no inhibitions about display, with the result that architecture was often extremely ostentatious. Absence of civil strife made it possible to abandon all thoughts of defence in planning a country mansion, and this led to an opening up process with houses sometimes appropriately shaped like the letter "E", instead of looking inwards upon a courtyard. Renaissance influences brought with them a desire for classical symmetry – there is all the difference in the world, in this respect, between Compton Wynyates and Longleat. New-found wealth often expressed itself in excessive ornamentation: heavily carved panelling, elaborately worked plaster ceilings, and mullioned windows filled with armorial bearings in stained glass. It was all very grand, and rather fun; the Elizabethans liked it that way.

NON SINE SOLE IRIS.

Elizabeth I, the 'Rainbow' portrait at Hatfield House
by Zuccaro
(*By courtesy of the Marquess of Salisbury*)

ELIZABETH I, 1558–1603

(Daughter of HENRY VIII and Anne Boleyn, half-sister of EDWARD VI and MARY)

Born 1533, was 25 when she ascended the throne, and 69 when she died.

Thumbnail Sketch   A vital, calculating female, with a brilliant understanding of how to lead and manage Englishmen.

WHAT TO REMEMBER

Elizabeth's first task was the settlement of England's religious affairs. Her own utterances upon matters of belief are obscure, but her policy and that of her minister William Cecil (later Lord Burleigh) was the establishment of a "via media". A new Act of Supremacy (1559) pronounced her "Supreme Governor", an appellation more acceptable to Catholics than Henry VIII's "Supreme Head", while an Act of Uniformity (1559) restored Edward VI's Second Prayer Book, with certain changes calculated to decrease its offensiveness to catholic susceptibilities, and enjoined compulsory church attendance with fines for absentees. This legislation determined the character of Anglicanism from that day to this, but failed to embrace sincere Roman Catholics on the one hand or the growing element of Calvinist Puritans and presbyterians on the other.

Foreign affairs presented delicate problems. Mary Stuart, married to Francis II of France, claimed the English throne by virtue of being great-granddaughter to Henry VII, while Philip II of Spain made Elizabeth offers of marriage, preoccupied with the dangers which Valois domination of England spelt for the Hapsburgs. Elizabeth assisted, first secretly, then openly, the presbyterian anti-French elements in Scotland, with the result that when the widowed Mary returned to her kingdom in 1561 she found a situation, religious and political, which was distasteful to her, and that she constituted in her own person a potential rallying point for disaffected Catholics against her cousin of England. So started the complicated and melancholy tale which culminated in Mary's execution at Fotheringay in 1587. Meanwhile relations with Spain deteriorated. Ebullient English seamen buccaneered amongst Spanish Caribbean possessions (with secret regal assistance); English Catholics – encouraged by their Queen's excommunication (1570) and enflamed by gallant Jesuit missionaries – plotted with Spaniards to assassinate their ruler; Elizabeth – with an eye to markets – assisted the Netherlands rebels against Philip (Sir Philip Sidney died at Zutphen in 1586); England and Spain eventually found themselves openly at war, and Sir Francis Drake and the weather scattered the Armada in 1588, hostilities continuing until the end of the reign.

The names of Frobisher, Davis, Hawkins, Raleigh and Drake evoke memories of exploration, colonization and naval glory; William Cecil, Sir Francis Walsingham and Robert Cecil stand for statesmanship, Leicester and Essex for amatory intrigue and courtly elegance; music and literature sparkle with the genius of Tallis, Byrd, Orlando Gibbons, Spenser, Raleigh, Sidney, Marlowe, Shakespeare and Jonson – yet all was not glory under "Gloriana". Unemployment, rising prices, the decay of ancient towns and of agriculture caused acute social problems, and an attempt was made to deal with these by the Statute of Apprentices (1563) and the great Poor Law of 1601 which was to last until 1834. Parliament too, growing conscious of its strength, was not always at one with its royal mistress. But Elizabeth's genius lay in her capacity for managing Englishmen. "And though you

have had, and may have, many Princes more mighty and wise sitting in this seat, yet you never had, or shall have, any that will be more careful and loving", she said in 1601. In 1603 she died.

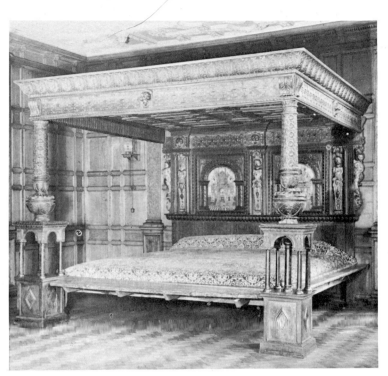

The Great Bed of Ware

(Victoria and Albert Museum. Crown Copyright)

JACOBEAN
1603–1625

James I   1603–1625

JACOBEAN
Blickling Hall
(*By permission of the National Trust*)

JACOBEAN

1603–1625

Jacobean architecture does not differ greatly from Elizabethan. The emphasis is still on the secular rather than on the ecclesiastical, houses are still grand, but with a rather simpler grandeur, and there is a new tendency to use, to some extent, the Doric, Ionic and Corinthian orders. Blickling Hall, in Norfolk, provides a charming example of the style of the period.

James I, by Daniel Mytens
(*By permission of the National Portrait Gallery*)

JAMES I, 1603–1625

(Son of Mary, Queen of Scots, and Darnley. Great-great-grandson of HENRY VII, through the latter's daughter Margaret
who married James IV of Scotland)

Born 1566, was 36 when he ascended the throne, and 58 when
he died.

Married Anne of Denmark, and had two sons:
Henry, who died in 1612
CHARLES I
and a daughter Elizabeth, who married Frederick, the Elector
Palatine. Their twelfth child, Sophia, became Electress of
Hanover, to whom "and the heirs of her body being Protestant"
the crown of England was to pass by the Act of Settlement of
1701.

Thumbnail Sketch "The wisest fool in Christendom."

WHAT TO REMEMBER

From Scotland came a learned, mixed-up, raffish absolutist –
James I. The opportunist Tudors had left English institutions in
a state of unstable equilibrium, the first two Stuarts, lacking
their predecessors' common touch, drove the country to Civil
War. None of the problems – religious, parliamentary, financial
and foreign political – was insoluble, but they could not be
solved without radical change, either absolutist or constitutional-
ist, and they all contributed to the 1642 catastrophe.

English Puritans and Catholics looked optimistically to James I,
the former because of his upbringing in presbyterian Scotland, the
latter because of his mother's faith. The Hampton Court Conference (1604), with James' explosive "No bishop, no king,"
disappointed Puritan hopes, indirectly driving the Pilgrim
Fathers to New England (1620), but achieved the Authorized
Translation of the Bible (1604–1611). Meanwhile the Catholics,
dissatisfied that James, having suspended the Penal Laws under
which they had suffered since 1571, did not proceed to complete
toleration, resorted to plotting. The conspiracies of Watson and
Cobham brought retribution which stimulated the Gunpowder

Treason of 5 November 1605 – a murderous enterprise which discredited the old religion for years to come.

Parliament, not yet recognized as permanent and essential, might yet have suffered the fate of the French States General, which did not meet from 1615 to 1789, had it not been for James' financial crises. Even Elizabeth had had to exercise skilful charm in managing this institution; James, totally uncomprehending of what he was up against, observed that "the state of monarchy is the supremest thing on earth", warned his Commons not to "debate publicly of matters far above their reach and capacity" and, when a deputation called upon him, treated them as foreigners with the phrase: "set stools for the ambassadors". Parliament, however, held its own, and England was spared the authoritarianism which gripped continental Europe.

Finance was the key. There was a vast rise of prices between 1580 and 1640, largely caused by the influx of precious metal from the New World, and James was wildly extravagant. Had the Great Contract, brain-child of Robert Cecil, Earl of Salisbury, whereby the crown was to forgo its right to ancient feudal dues for an annual grant of £200,000, been acceptable to Parliament, the problem might have been solved. But Parliament appreciated the power of the purse, James and his son were forced to increasingly unpopular methods of money-raising, and the end was violent.

Religion, relations with Parliament, and finance played their part in foreign policy. James, "Rex Pacificus", concluded peace

with catholic Spain in 1604, but married his daughter Elizabeth to the protestant Elector Palatine in 1613. He was, for years, deeply influenced by Gondomar, the Spanish Ambassador (to please whom Raleigh was executed in 1618) and who encouraged the King to pursue the chimera of a match between Charles and the Infanta Maria – a stroke by which James hoped to recoup his finances and, later, to restore the Palatinate to his son-in-law Frederick, whose hereditary dominions had been occupied by the Spaniards in the opening stages of the Thirty Years War. But England idolized the Electoral pair, and wished to fight for them – bonfires

blazed and London roared when Charles returned from Madrid a bachelor, war was declared on Spain, and a scarcely less fateful betrothal arranged between the heir to the throne and Henrietta Maria of France.

Harassed, weary and a failure, James died in March 1625.

STUART

1625–1702

Charles I	1625–1649
Commonwealth	1649–1660
Charles II	1660–1685
James II	1685–1689
William and Mary	1689–1694
William III	1694–1702

STUART

Queen's House, Greenwich
(By permission of the Trustees, National Maritime Museum)

Trinity College, Cambridge, Wren's Library
(By permission of the Royal Commission on Historical Monuments)

STUART

1625–1702

With the Stuart period individual architects come into their own and the two great names are Inigo Jones (1573–1651) and Sir Christopher Wren (1632–1723). Inigo Jones travelled and studied in Italy and fell under the influence of the work of Palladio (1508–1580), hence the introduction of a true Renaissance "Palladian" style here. As Surveyor-General of Royal Buildings (a post subsequently held by Wren) he accomplished work of a purity and academic correctness which found many imitators. Wren, his illustrious successor, one who could develop the Italian into something truly English, showed increased flexibility and richness – compare Queen's House, Greenwich, by Jones, with Wren's library at Trinity College, Cambridge. Both these men were giants, and the period one of great architectural distinction.

Charles I, equestrian statue by Le Sueur at Charing Cross
(*By permission of Pitkin Pictorials Ltd*)

CHARLES I, 1625–1649

(Son of JAMES 1 and Anne of Denmark)

Born 1600, was 24 when he ascended the throne, and 48 when he died.

Married Henrietta Maria of France and had three sons:
CHARLES II   Henry, Duke of Gloucester
JAMES II   (1639–1660)
and three daughters:
Mary – married William II of Orange
Elizabeth (died 1650)
Henrietta – married Philip of Orleans.

Thumbnail Sketch   A cultivated gentleman who never kept his word in politics.

WHAT TO REMEMBER

The reign of Charles I, which unfolds with the inevitability of tragedy, might have been that of Henry IX. James I's powerful elder son, who died in 1612, had the qualities of the successful despot, which could have changed the course of English history.

The years 1625–1629 saw Charles' marriage with Henrietta Maria, three parliaments, war with Spain and France and, until his assassination by Felton in 1628, the domination of the Duke of Buckingham. Parliament, international in outlook and fearing autocracy on the European pattern, counting among its members the formidable John Pym and Sir John Eliot, was intransigent about finance, eager to impeach the militarily incompetent Buckingham, and continually at loggerheads with its monarch. The Petition of Right (1628) condemned forced loans, arbitrary imprisonment, the billeting of soldiers on the people, and martial law, and, before the adjournment of 1629, the Speaker was held in his chair while a resolution was passed that innovators in religion and those who levied or paid taxes not sanctioned by Parliament were enemies of England.

A period of non-parliamentary government, frequently miscalled "The Eleven Years of Tyranny" (1629–1640), followed. Thomas Wentworth, later Earl of Strafford, earned the enmity of the Commons by deserting them and putting his "Thorough" administrative genius at the disposal of the monarchy, first in northern England, subsequently in Ireland. William Laud, meticulous and donnish Archbishop of Canterbury, roused against Charles, more than any other single person, powerful elements inimical to the imposition of High Anglican uniformity. Sir John Eliot died in the Tower, William Prynne lost his ears for attacking episcopacy, John Hampden refused payment of Ship Money, Puritan emigration to New England proceeded apace, but the Courts of Star Chamber and High Commission were mild compared with the despotic machinery of France and Spain. Straitened finance forbad war and, generally, life proceeded pleasantly until Laud and Charles attempted to force an Anglican Prayer Book on the Scots. This stimulated Jenny Geddes to hurl her stool at the Dean of St. Giles's and provoked the two Bishops' Wars (1639 and 1640), leaving a Scottish army in England, paid for by the King.

This crisis necessitated the recall of Parliament – the Short Parliament (April – May 1640), the Long Parliament in November. The pace immediately became hectic. Laud was imprisoned, Strafford, condemned by Bill of Attainder, died gallantly, the Courts of Star Chamber and High Commission were abolished, the Triennial Act (Parliament to be called every three years) went through, Charles agreed that the present Parliament should

not be dissolved without its own consent, and the Grand Remonstrance (201 objections to Charles' governmental methods) was passed. In January 1642 the King attempted, ill-advisedly and unsuccessfully, to arrest five members of the Commons, and withdrew from his capital.

The Civil War (1642–1646), a division on issues of conscience rather than class, was won by Parliament because of its superior financial resources, the support of the Navy and of London, and the military genius of Oliver Cromwell. In May 1646 Charles surrendered to the Scots and they, in January 1647,

Photograph by A. F. Kersting

Charles I's cradle at Hatfield House
(*By courtesy of the Marquess of Salisbury*)

handed him over to Parliament.

But Army and Parliament fell out – arrears of pay and fear of a new presbyterian uniformity, entertained by soldiers recruited from the Independent sects, were the causes. Lest Parliament should use the King, Cromwell kidnapped him (June 1647), Charles escaped and intrigued with the Scots, the latter marched south to defeat by Cromwell at Preston (August 1648) and Colonel Pride purged the Commons of its presbyterian members, leaving a "Rump" of some 100 Independents.

There remained the problem of the King – to which Cromwell saw a solution, cruel but necessary. The trial was a tragic farce, the end (30 January 1649) a scene of noble courage.

Oliver Cromwell, by Robert Walker
(*By permission of the National Portrait Gallery*)

COMMONWEALTH, 1649-1660

No King here – but of course one asks oneself, "Was Oliver Cromwell descended from Henry VIII's Thomas Cromwell?" The answer is "No", but there was a connection. An ancestor of Oliver, one Morgan Williams, married a sister of Thomas Cromwell. Morgan Williams' son took the name of his uncle Thomas, who was also his patron.

WHAT TO REMEMBER

England was now a Commonwealth, not a Kingdom, governed by a Council of State and the "Rump" – some thirty members of the latter sitting in the former. But, in Ireland and Scotland, men declared for Charles II.

Cromwell crossed St. George's Channel to slaughter the adherents of the Royalist Marquess of Ormonde at Drogheda and Wexford—to him "a marvellous great mercy", to subsequent generations "the curse of Cromwell" (1649). Next year he transferred to Scotland, where the young King had landed, was victorious at Dunbar (3 September) and occupied Edinburgh. In 1651 a Scottish army marched south, pursued by Cromwell, who, again on 3 September, defeated them at Worcester, after which "Charles Stuart, a long dark man" was on the run from Boscobel Oak to the Adur estuary, eventually escaping to Fécamp.

At sea the great admiral Robert Blake defeated Prince Rupert, king's cavalryman turned sailor (1649–1652), and then switched to the Dutch. This war, precipitated by the 1651 Navigation Act, which forbad the import of goods from Europe in any but English ships or those of the producer country, was a ding-dong two year struggle between Van Tromp, de Ruyter and Blake, ending in victory for the latter.

At home the government's unpopularity had increased, particularly in Army circles, a crisis arising over the "Perpetuation Bill", empowering members of the "Rump" to veto members elected to the next Parliament. Cromwell and thirty soldiers stopped this – the words "You are no parliament", the reference to the mace as "this bauble" are famous; the Long Parliament was no more. A predominantly military council selected 129 "Saints" for a short-lived Parliament, taking its name from "Praise God Barbon" (1653). Revolutionary and unsatisfactory, the "Saints" were persuaded to resign by Army officers who now presented Cromwell with "The Instrument of Government", declaring him Lord Protector, ruling with a Council of State and a Parliament. But Protectors, like Kings, find parliaments difficult – this one survived four months. Cromwell now tried the short and grimly unsuccessful experiment of dividing the country into eleven districts, governed by moralizing Major-Generals, who took a lot of fun out of life, but killed militarism in England for ever. Another Parliament followed, offering Cromwell the crown by "The Humble Petition and Advice" (1657), but misunderstandings made this Parliament, also, short-lived.

The Commonwealth had greatness, with all its troubles: tolerant of religion – except for "popery or prelacy" – bold in foreign policy, capturing Jamaica from Spain (1655) and, with the French, taking Spanish-owned Dunkirk in 1658, but imposing an unbearable strain on Cromwell. He died, aged 59, in that year – the date was 3 September.

Five months rule by Cromwell's son Richard, "Tumbledown Dick", reduced England to chaos. The situation was saved by General Monk's march from Scotland to London, his restoration of the Long Parliament, its self-dissolution and the formation of

the Convention Parliament of 1660, which invited Charles II home.

Silver Cup (1652)
(*By permission of the Warden and Fellows of Winchester College*)

Charles II, attributed to John Michael Wright
(*By permission of the National Portrait Gallery*)

CHARLES II, 1660–1685

(Son of CHARLES I and Henrietta Maria)

Born 1630, returned to Whitehall on his 30th birthday, and was 54 when he died.

Married Catherine of Braganza, but had no legitimate children.

Thumbnail Sketch   An amorous comedian, the wide range of whose activities seldom included his duty, but *really* able.

WHAT TO REMEMBER

On 25 May 1660 a foreign looking gentleman landed at Dover. The mayor presented him with a Bible; Charles II was back. He was bound by his Declaration of Breda to pardon all not excepted by Parliament, to permit liberty of conscience to those who kept the peace, to accept Parliament's land settlement, and discharge the arrears due to Monk's army. The emphasis was on Parliament now and forever. There were some executions, mainly of regicides, and the distasteful violation of the corpses of Cromwell, Ireton and Bradshaw. Cavaliers recovered confiscated lands, but those whose acres had been sold to meet taxation went uncompensated; Crown and Church recovered all Monk's army was paid off, except for two regiments (later the Coldstream and the Blues), and Charles was granted £1,200,000 annually. In December the Convention Parliament was dissolved.

May 1661 saw the Cavalier Parliament, which lasted until 1679. Back came Church and Prayer Book, supported by the Clarendon Code (1661–5), unjustly attributed to Charles' chief minister Edward Hyde, Earl of Clarendon, which laid disabilities – religious, social, educational and political – on Nonconformists, creating a cleavage in England which has died hard.

Meanwhile Charles, in 1662, made two profitable transactions: marriage with Catherine of Braganza, bringing Bombay, Tangier and a splendid dowry, and the sale of Dunkirk to Louis XIV, after which the country embarked upon another Dutch War (1664–7) – a harsh period including the Great Plague (1665), the Great Fire (1666), fleet mutinies, de Ruyter in the Medway and, finally, the Peace of Breda, gaining us New Amsterdam (renamed

New York) and New Jersey. In 1667 Clarendon fell, scapegoat for an inglorious war and resented for the marriage of his daughter Anne with James, Duke of York. The "Cabal" ministry (Clifford, Arlington, Buckingham, Ashley-Cooper, Lauderdale) replaced his.

Abroad Louis XIV, absolute monarch of populous and bellicose France, started his first aggressive war – in the Spanish Netherlands. England joined Holland and Sweden in the short-lived Triple Alliance against him (1668), but in 1670 Charles and Louis, through the agency of the former's sister and latter's sister-in-law Henrietta, concluded the Secret Treaty of Dover, whereby Charles was handsomely paid to support Louis' forthcoming attack on Holland and for undertaking, with doubtful sincerity, to declare himself a Catholic and restore the old faith. Thus (1672–4) England fought a third Dutch War, Charles issued a Declaration of Indulgence repealing all acts against Nonconformists and Catholics, Parliament insisted on its withdrawal and countered with the Test Act, restricting crown offices to Anglican communicants, which made his brother James, Duke of York, resign his naval command.

The Cabal was replaced (1673) by Sir Thomas Osborne, later Lord Danby, who mobilized supporters of Church and Court into a party subsequently named "Tory", while ex-Cabalist Ashley-Cooper, now Lord Shaftesbury, exploited the fear of

absolutism and the anti-catholic prejudice which animated the "Whigs", as the opposing faction came to be called. Titus Oates terrified England by his fantastic "Popish Plot" (1678–80), heads fell, Charles dissolved the Cavalier Parliament to save Danby from impeachment, but the next Parliament imprisoned him.

Charles' last five years saw the Habeas Corpus Act (1679), abortive Whig attempts to substitute his bastard son the Duke of Monmouth for his brother, the Duke of York, as heir to the throne (Exclusion Bill),

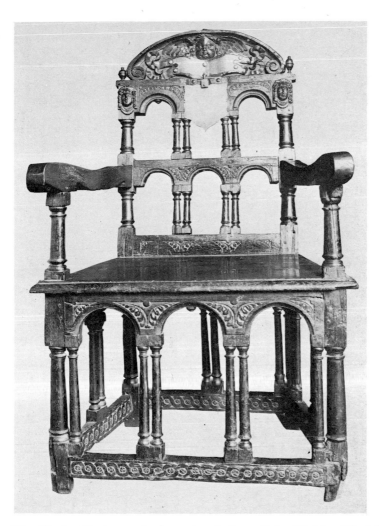

The Drake Chair, made from the timber of the 'Golden Hind,' when she was broken up, and given to the Bodleian Library in 1662 by John Davies of Camberwell, Keeper of Naval Stores at Deptford dockyard. *(By courtesy of the Bodleian Library)*

and the temporary downfall of Whiggery because of implication in the Rye House Plot to murder Charles and James (1683).

In 1685 Charles died, fortified by the rites of the Church which he had failed to restore.

James II, by Sir Godfrey Kneller
(*By permission of the National Portrait Gallery*)

JAMES II, 1685–1688

(Son of CHARLES I and Henrietta Maria, brother of CHARLES II)

Born 1633, was 51 when he ascended the throne, and 55 when he fled the country.

Married Anne Hyde, and had two daughters:
> MARY, who married William of Orange
> ANNE

Thereafter married Mary of Modena, and had one son:
> James, the Old Pretender

Thumbnail Sketch   Serious and courageous professional soldier, unattractively sensual, the worst of the Stuarts at managing Englishmen.

WHAT TO REMEMBER

Despite the Exclusion Bill troubles, James II succeeded his brother without incident, and received generous financial treatment from Parliament. His illegitimate nephew, the Duke of Monmouth, however, landed at Lyme Regis in June, proclaimed himself King at Taunton, was defeated at Sedgemoor, and executed, leaving his followers to rough handling by Colonel Kirke's "lambs" and the "Bloody Assize" of Judge Jeffreys.

James, encouraged by these events, now pressed on to the achievement of two objects – the restoration of catholicism and the establishment of absolutism. Englishmen viewed with alarm their King's approval of Louis XIV's revocation of the Edict of Nantes, and, after the prorogation of Parliament in November 1685, his use of the Dispensing Power to override the Test Act and confer upon his co-religionists important appointments – military, governmental, ecclesiastical and academic. It was madness to incur the enmity of the Anglican Church and the Tories, the Stuarts' staunchest supports, but that is what James did, enforcing church discipline by a new Ecclesiastical Commission and attempting to intimidate London by the summer camps of his formidable standing army on Hounslow Heath.

In April 1687, moving towards his religious objective and attempting to attract friends, James issued a Declaration of Indulgence for Catholics and Dissenters. This was repeated a year later, followed by an order commanding its reading in all churches. In May 1688 Archbishop Sancroft, supported by six bishops of the Province of Canterbury, petitioned the King against this, whereupon James sued them for the publication of a seditious libel. The only comfort for England was that the reign would not last for ever, and that James' daughters by Anne Hyde, Mary and Anne, were Protestants. On 10 June the Queen, Mary of Modena, gave birth to a son. The cry that the infant was supposititious and the swift circulation of the warming-pan rumour bear witness to the anxiety of the times. But, on 30 June, the Bishops were acquitted and a sinister sound rang in the King's ears – the soldiers were cheering on Hounslow Heath.

At this juncture seven important persons, Whig and Tory, signed an invitation asking William of Orange to invade England and overthrow the King. In November he landed at Torbay, and James concentrated a powerful force at Salisbury. Discouraged, however, by defection and desertion, James fled, was captured, and permitted to escape, eventually joining his Queen and son in France. Early in 1689, on conditions laid down in the Declaration of Rights, a Convention offered the throne to William and Mary as joint sovereigns – the unattractive,

asthmatic and powerful prince, curiously idolized by his wife, would accept no less, and the "Glorious Revolution" was over.

Glass Goblet and Cover
(*Victoria and Albert Museum. Crown Copyright*)

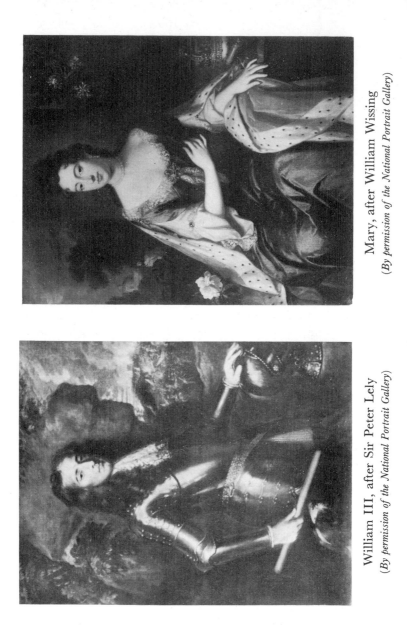

William III, after Sir Peter Lely
(By permission of the National Portrait Gallery)

Mary, after William Wissing
(By permission of the National Portrait Gallery)

WILLIAM and MARY, 1689–94
WILLIAM III, 1694–1702

(WILLIAM was the son of William II of Orange and Mary, daughter of CHARLES I. MARY was elder daughter of JAMES II and Anne Hyde)

WILLIAM, born 1650, was 38 when he ascended the throne, and 51 when he died. MARY, born 1662, was 26 when she ascended the throne, and 32 when she died.
WILLIAM and MARY had no children.

Thumbnail Sketch (*William*)   Cold unattractive man, second-rate soldier of immense tenacity, able diplomat and architect of alliances.

WHAT TO REMEMBER

Dutch William, liberty's unglamorous champion, had opposed Louis XIV implacably since the latter's invasion of Holland in 1672. He valued England primarily as a card in this game, and we were at war with France (League of Augsburg) from early 1689, though preoccupations in the British Isles prevented William's return to the continent before 1690. The Bill of Rights, embodying the Declaration of Rights, gave Parliament control over finance and the army, freedom in elections, freedom of speech, and laid emphasis on frequent meeting – a principle regularized by the Triennial Act (1695), whereby no Parliament was to sit for *more* than three years and had to be called at least *once* in three years. At the same time press censorship lapsed and the power to "suspend" laws was withdrawn. In the religious sphere an Act of Succession stipulated that the monarch might neither embrace catholicism nor marry a Romanist, though a governmental blind eye gave members of the old faith considerable unofficial liberty in observance. The Toleration Act allowed freedom of worship to protestant nonconformists, but municipal offices and crown appointments were reserved for Anglican communicants. Yet there was "establishment" opposition and six bishops, with some 400 lower clergy (Non-Jurors), refused the oaths of allegiance and supremacy, and lost their posts.

The Revolution Settlement betokened a decline in royal power, but William, ruling alone after Mary's death (1694), was no puppet-king. Scotland found satisfaction in the newly established Presbyterian Kirk (1690), though Highland resentment was demonstrated by Graham of Claverhouse, "Bonny Dundee", who beat the English and fell at Killiecrankie (1689). This resentment was intensified by the Glencoe massacre (1692), for which William, though probably inadequately informed, must bear some responsibility. James II's discomfiture in Ireland, by the relief of Londonderry (1689) and by defeat at the Battle of the Boyne (1690), still provides excuse for alcoholic celebration by Orangemen, but spelt years of economic and religious tyranny over Irish Catholics. Nonetheless the base was secured and William could turn to Europe and serve his vital interests by diplomatic genius and mediocre military talent.

The War of the League of Augsburg (1688–1697), with William uniting most of Europe against France, makes depressing military reading, enlivened by the allied naval victory off La Hogue (1692), (our first success in a struggle which would end with Trafalgar). War also led to the foundation of the Bank of England (1694), to meet the financial strain of prolonged hostilities, and culminated in the Peace of Ryswick which, at least, secured Dutch occupation of certain Netherlands fortresses and Louis' recognition of William as King of England, with his sister-in-law Anne as heiress.

Eyes now turned on Spain, where the childless Charles II lay dying. William had tried to assure the future balance of power by two Partition Treaties with Louis XIV (1698, 1700), dividing the Spanish inheritance between the Bourbons and the Hapsburgs. Charles II died (1700) leaving the whole to Philip of Anjou, Louis XIV's grandson. War became inevitable when Louis, accepting the will, seized the Netherlands' fortresses, and, when James II died, (September 1701) recognised his son, the Old Pretender, as James III, despite the Ryswick agreement

William and Mary Secretaire
(From Old English Furniture *by Hampden Gordon (John Murray)
by permission of Mrs Hampden Gordon)*

and the Act of Settlement (June 1701), which passed the English crown after William and Anne, to the Electress Sophia of Hanover and "the heirs of her body being Protestants" (see page 131).

May 1702 brought the War of the Spanish Succession, wherein the Grand Alliance (England, Holland, the Empire) opposed France. But the Alliance lacked its creator – William's horse had stumbled over a Hampton Court molehill. The King's broken collar-bone was followed by pleurisy and, on 8 March, he had died.

GEORGIAN

1702–1830

Photograph by Ursula Hamilton

GEORGIAN
Bedford Square, London

GEORGIAN

1702–1830

"The Age of Elegance" (elegance tempered by Hogarth, one might say) produced a crop of distinguished architects. You may well meet the following names: Nicholas Hawksmoor (1661–1736), Sir John Vanbrugh (1664–1726), James Gibbs (1682–1754), William Kent (1684–1748), George Dance (1700–1768, and his son George), John Wood (1705–1754, and his son John), Sir William Chambers (1726–1796), Robert Adam (1728–1792, and his brother William), Thomas Leverton (1743–1824) and John Nash (1752–1835).

Hawksmoor and Vanbrugh were both exponents of the baroque – the former specialized in churches, while the latter (soldier, dramatist and herald as well as architect) might well today have employed his highly developed theatrical sense on the design of film sets. The period saw great houses like Blenheim (Vanbrugh) and Stowe (Adam), it was an era of town planning producing splendid streets, squares (e.g. Bedford Square by Leverton), terraces and crescents – by the Dances in Dublin, the Woods in Bath and the Adams in London. Within these houses was set the furniture of Chippendale, Hepplewhite and Sheraton. As well as eighteenth century reasonableness there was the romance of the bogus ruin, a certain amount of neo-Gothic, the extravagance of chinoiserie, and one remembers that John Nash was not only responsible for Carlton House Terrace and a large number of "*cottages ornés*" but also for the Pavilion at Brighton.

Anne, by Michael Dahl
(*By permission of the National Portrait Gallery*)

ANNE, 1702–1714

(Daughter of JAMES II and Anne Hyde, sister of MARY)

Born 1665, was 37 when she ascended the throne, and 49 when she died.

Married Prince George of Denmark – a happy marriage marred by many miscarriages and deaths in infancy.

Thumbnail Sketch Religious, virtuous, dull, obstinate, a prey to ill-health – but kindly withal, and popular.

WHAT TO REMEMBER

The personality of "Good Queen Anne" may fail to capture the imagination, but her reign is packed with events of great significance for our historical development, while its hard-fought political battles live in the writings of Defoe, Swift, Addison, Steele and Pope. Her first ministry (1702–1710), headed by Lord Godolphin, started as a Whig-Tory combination, with the Duke and Duchess of Marlborough, whose elder daughter had married Godolphin's son, exploiting to the full their position as royal favourites. The War of the Spanish Succession was prosecuted energetically. The Methuen Treaty (1709), imposing the light duty of £7 5s. 3d. per tun on Portuguese wines (as against £55 5s. od. on French), led Englishmen eventually to Dr Swizzle's comforting belief that "a pint of old Port and a devilled biscuit can hurt no man", while Sir George Rooke's capture of Gibraltar (1704), with the Spanish garrison conveniently diverted by a Saint's Day mass, had direct influence on the subsequent triumphs of the British Navy. Then, sounding like a roll of distant drums, came the victories of Marlborough, England's greatest captain: Blenheim (1704), Ramillies (1706), Oudenarde (1708) and Malplaquet (1709). In Spain one recalls an interesting campaign by Lord Peterborough and the defeat of an Anglo-Portuguese force at Almanza (1707) by the Duke of Berwick, an illegitimate nephew of Marlborough, being the bastard son of James II by the Duke's sister, Arabella Churchill. Meanwhile, at home, the Union of England and Scotland was effected in 1707, with the Parliaments merged, though Scotland kept her Presbyterian national church and her own law, the latter providing many generations of eloping English couples with the romantic facilities of Gretna Green. In 1708 the Godolphin ministry rid itself of its Tory element in the persons of Robert Harley and Henry St. John, formidable characters who now hastened to take advantage of the Queen's innate detestation of the Whigs. While Harley's cousin Abigail Hill (Mrs Masham) wormed her way into the position of Queen's confidante, hitherto held by the Duchess of Marlborough, these two subtle politicians plotted. The ministry, already unpopular with a war-weary nation (they had refused Louis' peace offer after Oudenarde) made the error of impeaching the High Church Dr Sacheverell (1710) for sermons which abused the government's failure to uphold the interests of the ecclesiastical establishment. Great popular enthusiasm greeted the Doctor's token sentence: he was merely forbidden to preach for three years (1710).

In this same year Anne was delighted to dismiss the Whigs, and in came the Tories led by Harley, now Earl of Oxford, and St. John, now Lord Bolingbroke. Peace was their policy. Marlborough was sent packing, his successor, the Duke of Ormonde, remained quietly on the defensive until, in 1713, hostilities ended with the Treaty of Utrecht. From this Great Britain gained substantial advantages: Gibraltar, Minorca, Newfoundland, Nova Scotia and territory near Hudson Bay – above all the war brought

us great naval power and a humbled France. The Queen, however, had not long to live and the Whigs were already in close communication with George Louis, Elector of Hanover, son of the Electress Sophia. Bolingbroke now ousted Oxford, but Anne died before he could consolidate his position. The arrival of the Elector as George I restored the Whigs, and Bolingbroke threw in his lot with James, the exiled "Old Pretender" whom, perhaps, he would have welcomed as King.

Silver Chocolate Pot
(*Victoria and Albert Museum. Crown Copyright*)

George I, Studio of Sir Godfrey Kneller
(*By permission of the National Portrait Gallery*)

GEORGE I, 1714–1727

(Great-grandson of JAMES I)

Born 1660, was 54 when he ascended the throne, and 67 when he died.

Married Sophia Dorothea of Celle, whom he divorced in 1694 as a result of the Königsmark scandal, and who spent the rest of her life incarcerated at Ahlden. They had one son:

GEORGE II

and one daughter, Sophia Dorothea, who married Frederick William I of Prussia and became the mother of Frederick the Great.

Thumbnail Sketch A very unattractive German who disliked England, but possessed the virtue of courage.

WHAT TO REMEMBER

On 8 June 1714 that formidable bluestocking the Electress Sophia of Hanover collapsed and died in the park at Herrenhausen, predeceasing Queen Anne by about two months. The crown of England thus passed in accordance with the Act of Settlement of 1701 (see page 157) to Sophia's eldest son, George Louis. "George in pudding time came o'er", knowing that the Whigs were the men for him, and the Court of St. James's suffered the influx of a number of dreary Teutons, of whom the King's mistresses – the Schulenburg and the Kielmansegge – the former thin as a "Maypole", the latter with "two acres of cheek" and "an ocean of neck" (Horace Walpole), were notorious. The Parliamentary title to the throne was emphasized as never before by the accession of this monarch.

Good intelligence about continental Jacobitism (support for James Edward, the Old Pretender) ensured that the Whig government (Stanhope, Sunderland, Townshend and Walpole) was not surprised by the rebellion of 1715. On 13 November two engagements took place: at Sheriffmuir

> "There's some say that we wan,
> Some say that they wan,
> Some say that nane wan at a', man."

But the Whig Duke of Argyll at least prevented the southward advance of that very amateur soldier the Earl of Mar while, almost two hundred miles away, an insignificant insurgent force capitulated at Preston. James himself did not appear in Scotland until January 1716, and stayed but a short while. His observation "For me it is no new thing to be unfortunate" was hardly a rallying cry, and his impolitic if high-minded determination not to renounce catholicism blighted his chances. Otherwise, except for certain operations against Spain (destruction of the Spanish Fleet at Cape Passaro in 1718, siege of Gibraltar 1727–8), the reign was peaceful, largely owing to the Triple Alliance of 1718 (England, France, Holland), the Quadruple Alliance of 1719 (England, France, Holland, Austria) and the death of the portentous Charles XII of Sweden in 1718, whose hostility to Hanover had led him to support the Jacobites.

The Whig government held Parliament in a firm grip by astute manipulation of "rotten boroughs" (where the handful of parliamentary electors could be bribed), of "pocket boroughs" (whose owners nominated members), and of the all important royal patronage, relinquished by a foreign King who was basically uninterested in England and English politics. These manoeuvres were facilitated by the passing of the Septennial Act (1716), which kept the existing Parliament in being for seven years

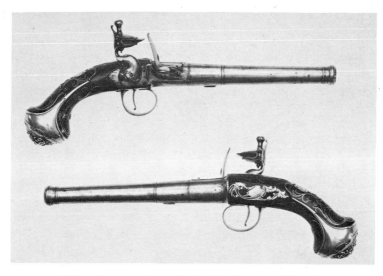

Pair of cannon-barrel pistols. Tower of London
(Ministry of Works. Crown Copyright Reserved)

instead of three and remained on the Statute Book until 1911.
Internal stresses put Walpole and Townshend out of the ministry
in 1717, but the failure of the South Sea Company (the financial
crash known as the "South Sea Bubble" – 1720), after which the
overstrained Stanhope died, did much to clear the way for their
return. In 1722, after Sunderland's death, Sir Robert Walpole–
ruthless, ambitious, tough, genial, a consummate politician and
much endeared to the monarch – became what today would be
called Prime Minister. George I was unintelligent and sadly
lacking in knowledge of English politics. These were more serious
defects than his inability to speak English – indeed there was no
lack of communication between him and Walpole. The attractive
myth of conferences in basic Latin will not stand up to the fact
that the Hanoverian and the Old Etonian could converse together
in perfectly adequate French. Walpole's gamekeeper's letters,
beagles and bottle did not affect his enormous capacity for work
and his priceless gift to England was the chance of peaceful
recovery after the great effort against Louis XIV. This had been
achieved, in great measure, when George I died in his coach on
the way to Hanover in 1727.

George II, by Thomas Hudson
(*By permission of the National Portrait Gallery*)

GEORGE II, 1727–1760

(Son of GEORGE I and Sophia Dorothea of Celle)

Born 1683, was 44 when he ascended the throne, and 77 when he died.

Married Caroline of Ansbach, and had three sons:
> Frederick, Prince of Wales (father of GEORGE III)
> George William (died in infancy)
> William Augustus, Duke of Cumberland

and five daughters.

Thumbnail Sketch A courageous but limited character, with a passion for money and detail. Mercifully influenced by a Queen who understood the wider issues of policy. Patron of Handel.

WHAT TO REMEMBER

George II had detested George I, so Walpole, essentially a George I man, was now dismissed. This indispensable minister, however, made a swift comeback with a tactfully substantial addition to "Dapper George's" Civil List and the consolidation of his position by close friendship with the able and attractive Queen, Caroline of Ansbach. He remained for almost fifteen years, withdrawing adroitly before the opposition which greeted his Excise Bill (1733) and pouring oil on the troubled waters of the Edinburgh Porteous Riots (1736). 1739 saw him unwillingly at war. The "Assiento" clause of the Treaty of Utrecht permitted our shipment of slaves to Spanish South America, restricting trade in other merchandise to one ship annually. Disregard of this regulation caused affrays on the Main and Captain Jenkins' grisly exhibition of his ear, allegedly lopped off by a Spanish official, aroused a public indignation which demanded hostilities.

War with Spain meant war with France, for the Bourbons of both countries were linked by the Family Compact (1733). A further complication was the War of the Austrian Succession (1740), precipitated by the young Frederick the Great of Prussia. He seized Silesia from the new Hapsburg Queen Maria Theresa of Austria, ignoring the Pragmatic Sanction which guaranteed her succession, and the chief combatants lined up: Prussia and France against England and Austria. George II, last English King to do so, led his troops at Dettingen (1743) and Lord Charles Hay did the famous courtesies of Fontenoy (1745). Walpole, no war leader, had resigned in 1742 and Henry Pelham had to withstand the shock of Charles Edward, the Young Pretender's "Forty-Five" rebellion. The Highlanders rose for this gallant figure, Sir John Cope was defeated at Prestonpans, the Prince penetrated to Derby, but withdrew owing to lack of English Jacobite support. In January 1746 he won the battle of Falkirk, but April saw the "waefu' day" of Culloden where Stuart hopes were shattered by the King's son, that "bluidy man", the Duke of Cumberland. The Highlands were subdued, Flora Macdonald typified the courage which kept Prince Charlie's secret and assisted that much loved young man to escape to the continent and the consolations of alcohol. In 1746 William Pitt, newly appointed Paymaster of the forces, gave our military administration a new look and, in 1748, the Treaty of Aix-la-Chapelle restored the "status quo ante bellum", giving Europe uneasy peace until 1756.

During England's repose Townshend, politician turned agriculturalist, began to revolutionize the countryside with his rotation of crops, Kay's flying shuttle (1733) heralded the Industrial Revolution, Dr Johnson's dictionary appeared (1755), John

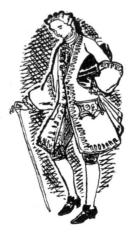

Pair of Silver Jugs (1732)
(By courtesy of the Ashmolean Museum)

Wesley preached throughout the land and society oscillated between the elegance of Lord Chesterfield and the genial coarseness of "Squire Western". But in India and North America English and French were at each others' throats while in Europe a "diplomatic revolution" reshuffled the pack, bringing together as allies in one camp Austria and France, in the other Prussia and England.

Frederick the Great, fearing for Silesia, opened the Seven Years War (1756–1763) by attacking Austria. Crisis brought William Pitt to the head of the ministry, justifiably confident that he alone could save England. Admiral Byng was shot for not relieving Minorca, Clive won at Plassey, Frederick the Great (subsidized by English gold) was victorious at Rossbach and Leuthen (all in 1757), the great year 1759 saw Wolfe's capture of Quebec, the French defeated by Admiral Hawke at Quiberon Bay and, on land, at Minden, with the result that, when George II died in October 1760, we dominated our foes in India, in North America and on the seas. In Europe the indefatigable Frederick fought grimly on.

George III, statue in Cockspur Street, London, by M. C. Wyatt

(*By courtesy of the National Buildings Record*)

GEORGE III, 1760–1820

(Son of Frederick, Prince of Wales and Augusta of Saxe-Gotha. Grandson of GEORGE II)

Born 1738, was 22 when he ascended the throne, 81 when he died.

Married Charlotte of Mecklenburg-Strelitz and had nine sons:

GEORGE IV	Ernest, Duke of Cumberland
Frederick, Duke of York	(King of Hanover, 1837–1857)
WILLIAM IV	Augustus, Duke of Sussex
Edward, Duke of Kent	Adolphus, Duke of Cambridge

    Octavius and Alfred who died young and unduked.

There were, also, six daughters.

Thumbnail Sketch A lover of England, albeit ambitious for the power of the crown, "Farmer George" was eventually loved by his subjects for his domesticity, his generosity and his courage. He patronized the arts and founded the Royal Academy (1768). His recurrent insanity evoked genuine sympathy.

WHAT TO REMEMBER

George III, unlike his grandfather and great-grandfather, "gloried in the name of Britain". and meant to follow maternal advice and "be a King". By 1770 six ministries had come and gone, the old entrenched Whig faction was out, Lord North was in (1770–1782) and Horace Walpole commented gloomily (1780) on the increased power of the crown. George had achieved this by recovering the royal patronage (the King's Friends) and by playing politics himself, eventually with North as his tool. Momentous events occurred. The Peace of Paris (1763) ended the Seven Years War, leaving us masters of Canada and triumphant in India (where the brilliant ruthlessness of Clive and Warren Hastings was soon to earn their country's ingratitude), while the Stamp Act (1765) started the great "No Taxation without Representation" row with the American Colonies which led, through the Boston Tea Riots (1773), Lexington and Bunker's Hill (1775), the Declaration of Independence (1776), war with France (1778), Spain (1779) and Holland (1780) to Cornwallis' surrender at Yorktown (1781) and the Peace of Versailles (1783), whereby we recognized the independence of the United States.

William Pitt, the elder, (later Chatham) had died in 1778. From 1783 to 1801 his son, the young Mr Pitt, headed a ministry increasingly Tory as time passed. Life was not dull. Warren Hastings was tried and acquitted (1788–1792), the King suffered his first serious mental breakdown (1788), in 1789 the noble George Washington became first President of the United States and, in France, the Bastille fell, causing Wordsworth to feel that "to be young was very heaven". Prussia and Austria moved against revolutionary France, the former withdrew from Valmy (1792) and Goethe proclaimed "a new epoch of world history". Louis XVI was guillotined (1793), England joined the ramshackle First Coalition against France, embracing Prussia, Austria, Spain and Holland. The parties to the coalition, preoccupied by the Second Partition of Poland, suffered reverses and fell apart in 1795. Lord Howe's naval victory of the First of June 1794 brightened the gloom, and England, disciplined by repressive anti-revolutionary legislation, fought on with Austria and Portugal. Napoleon Bonaparte (aged 27) defeated Austria brilliantly in Italy (1796–1797) and Nelson was victorious at Cape St. Vincent (1797). Next year Napoleon invaded Egypt, lost his fleet to Nelson (The Nile 1798) and returned home to become First Consul. A Second Coalition (1799) was as unsuccessful as the first (despite Abercromby's defeat of the French at Alexandria and Nelson's destruction of the Danish fleet at Copenhagen – 1801), and, during the same period, an Irish Rebellion (1798) was followed by the Act of Union (1800). One by one the powers made peace with France, England concluding the Treaty of Amiens in 1802.

In 1803 war was renewed and for two years Napoleon (Emperor 1804) threatened England with invasion. In 1805 Nelson defeated the French and Spanish at Trafalgar, Mr Pitt died in 1806, 1808–1813 saw Wellington's methodically

Pair of Hepplewhite chairs
(By courtesy of Mallett & Son, Ltd, 40 New Bond Street, London, W.1)

successful Peninsular campaign, meanwhile the Emperor added Austerlitz, Jena, Auerstadt, Wagram, etc., to his battle honours and proceeded to the cardinal error of 1812. The Grand Army reeled back across the snows from flaming Moscow, the heartened allies closed in, the Emperor abdicated and left, in April, 1814, for Elba. The powers, resettling Europe at the Congress of Vienna, were rudely shocked by Napoleon's reappearance in France but, in 1815, his glory departed at Waterloo and the Imperial sun set over St. Helena.

This long reign was one of vast development. Mechanization, achieved by the exploitation of coal, iron and steam began to change the face of England. Road engineers (e.g. Macadam) made great strides, canals were constructed. The population increased from 7 to 12 millions and many agricultural areas saw modernization by enclosure and the introduction of new techniques. Pain is inseparable from rapid growth and George III's closing years saw much unrest and distress of which the King, permanently mad since 1810, was happily oblivious.

George IV, by Sir Thomas Lawrence
(*By permission of the National Portrait Gallery*)

GEORGE IV, 1820–1830

(Son of GEORGE III and Charlotte of Mecklenburg-Strelitz)

Born 1762, was 57 when he ascended the throne, and 67 when he died.

Married Caroline of Brunswick (having previously married, without the King's consent, and therefore illegally, Mrs Fitzherbert) and had one daughter, Charlotte. The latter married Leopold of Saxe-Coburg, subsequently King of the Belgians. She died in childbirth.

Thumbnail Sketch   A gifted, educated, artistic profligate.

WHAT TO REMEMBER

With George III a pathetic, bearded lunatic at Windsor, his son, later George IV, had exercised the functions of Prince Regent since 1811. The greater part of his regency and reign is spanned by Lord Liverpool's Tory ministry (1812–1827), dominated first by Castlereagh and subsequently by Canning. In Vienna the Congress danced, upheld the claims of legitimacy and reaction, but ushered in a century during which Europe was little disturbed by war. Victorious Britain suffered unemployment and hunger. Unrest was general, the Habeas Corpus Act was suspended, the Blanketeers (so called from their portable sleeping equipment) made a famous protest march from Manchester (1817). Two years later the magistrates of that same city earned unthinking governmental congratulation by ordering a yeomanry unit to charge a mass meeting, causing eleven deaths and several hundred casualties (Peterloo 1819). The Six Acts of the same year brought further repression and, shortly after the new King's accession, there was discovered the Cato Street Conspiracy, of which the object was to murder the Cabinet. The reign, in fact, opened inauspiciously enough with this sinister plot, and the abortive attempt of George IV, whose own private life was hardly innocent of irregularities, to divorce his trollopy Queen, Caroline of Brunswick, by means of a Bill of Pains and Penalties. Indignity followed indignity: in 1821 the queen tried to break into George's coronation; she died, mercifully, shortly afterwards. In 1822 Castlereagh's coffin was carried to West-minster Abbey amidst scenes of public execration.

And now a happier era dawned. The great George Canning became Foreign Secretary in Castlereagh's place, with Robert Peel as Home Secretary, and William Huskisson as President of the Board of Trade. Canning refused Metternich's invitation to assist in the reactionary suppression of the Spanish Revolution of 1822 and made it quite clear that if Ferdinand VII of Spain, assisted by his ally France, tried to get back his colonies in Spanish South America, which had proclaimed themselves independent in Napoleonic days, the British navy would have to be reckoned with. Thus Canning, not unmindful of foreign markets, "called the New World into existence to redress the balance of the Old", while the United States President Monroe enunciated the well known doctrine which kept the hands of European colonialists off the American continents. This is also the time when classically minded Englishmen were stirred by the Greek War of Independence against the Turks, when Byron died at Missolonghi (1824), and when Admiral Codrington, dispatched with the object of mediation, and commanding a combined English, Russian and French force, sank the Turkish fleet in Navarino Bay (1827). At home Robert Peel greatly humanized a Penal Code, now generally recognized as barbarous, and went on to give London the blessing of a consciously unmilitary police force, soon to be copied throughout the land. Huskisson, tragically killed at the opening

of the Liverpool-Manchester railway in 1830 (the Stockton-Darlington line had been inaugurated five years previously), took certain preliminary steps towards Free Trade. Largely owing to the efforts of the enterprising radical tailor, Francis Place, the Combination Acts were repealed and Trade Unions became legal in 1824. Behind these reforms is discernible the thought and work of Jeremy Bentham and William Cobbett.

In February 1827 a stroke caused Lord Liverpool's resignation, Canning became Premier, but died six months later, and by January 1828 the Duke of Wellington was forming a Ministry.

Piano in rosewood with brass inlay, bought by George IV in 1822
(By courtesy of the Brighton Corporation: Royal Pavilion Committee)

The old soldier was not by nature a reformer, but Lord John Russell achieved the repeal of the Corporation and Test Acts (1828) which, at long last, gave nonconformists access to public office. The Clare Election of 1828, whereby Daniel O'Connell triumphed at the polls over Vesey-Fitzgerald, Wellington's nominee as President of the Board of Trade, but was unable to appear at Westminster because he was a member of the Church of Rome, led to the Catholic Emancipation Act of 1829.

Much had been accomplished, more was to come, and, clearly, Parliamentary Reform could not be withheld much longer. George IV died in June 1830, and the general election which followed this welcome event brought the essential change appreciably nearer.

VICTORIAN
1830–1901

| William IV | 1830–1837 |
| Victoria | 1837–1901 |

VICTORIAN
St. Pancras Station
(*By permission of British Railways*)

VICTORIAN

1830–1901

It would be unwise to belittle the achievements of the Victorian era in any field, and the feats of engineering accomplished in the erection of the enormous buildings required as a result of the Industrial Revolution (using iron, glass, etc., as in the Crystal Palace) are remarkable. However, this same revolution brought with it the drab workers' streets of Leeds, Sheffield and Manchester, from which horrors there was a thoroughly comprehensible desire to escape. Escape took the form of revivals – some saw truth and beauty in the Gothic, others in classical antiquity, typified in the one case by St. Pancras Station, and in the other by the old entrance to Euston. The Houses of Parliament, the Law Courts, and the buildings of many a public school gave infinite satisfaction to our forbears, who could agree with *The Daily Telegraph* that the Albert Memorial "is assuredly the most consummate and elegant piece of elegiac art which modern genius has produced".

William IV, by Sir Martin Archer Shee
(*By permission of the National Portrait Gallery*)

WILLIAM IV, 1830–1837

(Son of GEORGE III and Charlotte of Mecklenburg-Strelitz. Brother of GEORGE IV)

Born 1765, was 64 when he ascended the throne, and 71 when he died.

Married Adelaide of Saxe-Meiningen, but their two children died in infancy.

Thumbnail Sketch   A well-meaning, courageous naval officer, but an inept and timid politician.

WHAT TO REMEMBER

The reign of the genial, if eccentric, sailor who became William IV saw momentous happenings. For years forward-thinking minds had been exercised over Great Britain's ridiculous system of parliamentary representation – the uninhabited boroughs for which landowners nominated members, the "Rotten Boroughs" where the few electors could be bribed, the growing towns of the North which went entirely unrepresented – but fear of Jacobinism and preoccupation with a major war had held back the hands of the clock. In 1830 reform was in the air. The reactionary Charles X was driven from Paris and replaced by Louis Philippe, Belgium declared herself independent of Holland, there were liberal stirrings throughout Europe from Spain to Poland. In England, after the General Election of 1830, the Duke of Wellington, as Premier, declared: "The legislation and system of representation possesses the full and entire confidence of the country"— a sensational observation which led to his resignation and replacement by the Whig Lord Grey.

By 1 March 1831 the new Government was ready with a parliamentary Reform Bill, which passed its second reading by a majority of one and was later defeated. Parliament was dissolved, and the country proceeded to a General Election of rare excitement, during which voters who normally acted from motives of profit did the bidding of the mobs who roared around them, bringing the Whigs back with a majority of 136. The House of Commons was now sound, but obscurantist Tory opposition in the Lords led to Grey's resignation. Could Wellington step into this breach? Flames were flickering up and down the country and men were drilling in secret. Clearly it was a case of Grey with "the Bill, the whole Bill, and nothing but the Bill" – and when he returned, he carried an invincible weapon in the King's reluctant guarantee to create enough Whig peers •to see the measure through the Upper House, a step rendered unnecessary by the withdrawal of opposition by Wellington and his adherents. Thus, in June 1832, the great Reform Bill became law. Seats were taken away from anomalous constituencies and redistributed rationally, the vote was to be exercised, in the boroughs by householders paying £10 annual rent, in the counties by freeholders and leaseholders paying £10 a year on a long lease, or £50 on an annual lease. The aristocratic landowners had, in fact, gone into political partnership with the middle class.

Other reforms followed. 1807 had seen the end of the slave trade, in 1833 slavery was abolished within the British Empire. But work in the West Indian plantations, under a master who was, at least, interested in the physical survival of the labourer, may have been preferable to employment in an English factory, where children were virtually expendable. However, the Factory Act of 1833 forbad the employment of those under 9, restricted the hours of the 9–13 year-old to 48 per week, and those of the 13–18 year-old to 68. Above all, government inspectors were appointed to ensure that the Act was effective.

The Poor Law Amendment Act of 1834, inspired by Benthamite Utilitarianism, attacked the system devised by the Berkshire magistrates, meeting at the Pelican Inn, Speenhamland, Newbury in 1795, whereby inadequate wages were supplemented out of the rates. This well-meant scheme had encouraged meanness in employers and thriftlessness in the employed. Under the new act the able-bodied could only receive assistance in workhouses – where it was the duty of Mr Bumble and his colleagues to discourage applicants by ensuring that the arrangements were unattractive – which resulted

Silver Tea Pot
(*Victoria and Albert Museum. Crown Copyright*)

in much immediate misery even if, in the very long run, it helped
to bring about the payment of a living wage.

Parliamentary Reform had been a vital necessity; the same
was the case in local government, where for years medieval
muddle had obtained. Now the Municipal Corporations Act
(1835) gave ratepayers the right to elect a Council which, within
itself, produced its Mayor and Aldermen, to the great increase of
efficiency and integrity.

Meanwhile Grey had resigned (1834) and the premiership had
been held by Lord Melbourne (Whig), Sir Robert Peel
("Conservative" after the Tamworth Manifesto of 1834), and
Lord Melbourne again. Great events had occurred, great men
trod the stage, but, when William IV died on 20 June 1837, the
monarchy was held in low esteem. New glory was soon to shine
about it.

Victoria, by Sir George Hayter
(*By permission of the National Portrait Gallery*)

VICTORIA, 1837–1901

(Daughter of Edward, Duke of Kent, and Victoria Mary Louisa
of Saxe-Coburg-Saalfeld. Niece of WILLIAM IV)

Born 1819, was 18 when she ascended the throne, and 81 when
she died.

Married Albert of Saxe-Coburg-Gotha, and had four sons:
  EDWARD VII
  Alfred, Duke of Edinburgh and of Saxe-Coburg-Gotha
  Arthur, Duke of Connaught
  Leopold, Duke of Albany
and five daughters: Victoria, who married the Crown Prince of
Prussia and became the mother of the Emperor William II;
Princess Alice, who married the Grand Duke of Hesse; Princess
Helena (Princess Christian); Princess Louise, who married the
Duke of Argyll; and Princess Beatrice, who married Prince Henry
of Battenberg.

Thumbnail Sketch   "The girl, the wife, the aged woman, were the
same: vitality, conscientiousness, pride and simplicity were hers
to the latest hour." (Lytton Strachey).

WHAT TO REMEMBER

Early in the morning of 20 June 1837 the Archbishop of Canterbury and the Lord Chamberlain brought the news of the death
of William IV to a girl in Kensington Palace. Her diary records
a wish "to do what is fit and right". The great Victorian epoch
started. Some have smiled at it, none can laugh it off.

This tremendous reign was to see nineteen ministries, but, with
the exception of Disraeli, no Premier achieved so intimate a
relationship with the Queen as did the Whig Lord Melbourne.
He rendered signal service by initiating her into the mystery of
presiding "over the destinies of this great country", but his party
had already exhausted its reforming potentialities and, when
Melbourne resigned in 1841, Chartism, with its demands for
further Parliamentary reform, was a lively force. Sad as the Queen
was to see "Lord M" go, she now had the supreme comfort of
marriage with Prince Albert of Saxe-Coburg-Gotha (1840), which

made it easier for her to receive the Conservative Sir Robert
Peel. The major event of Peel's premiership (which also brought
it to a close) was the Repeal of the Corn Laws, (which had pro-
hibited the importation of foreign corn since 1815), precipitated
by the Irish potato famine of 1846. The forties saw further Acts,
associated with the name of Lord Shaftesbury, improving conditions in factories and mines; there was vast railway development.
The fifties celebrated the triumph of British prosperity in the
Great Exhibition (1851, brain child of the Prince Consort). With
all this went powerful activity – intellectual, literary and religious,
but not military. Yet England was about to become involved
in European war for the first time in almost forty years.

The Czar Nicholas I wished to profit from what he felt to be
the imminent disintegration of the Turkish Empire. England
feared Russia and therefore supported the Turkish "sick man".
The Emperor Napoleon III of France wanted alliance with
England and glory. Lord Aberdeen's government, with enthu-
siastic popular support, drifted into war, cause for which was
found in the Czar's claim to recognition as protector of all
Christians under Turkish rule. It took place in the Crimea
(1854–55), where the object was to capture Sebastópol, Russia's
chief naval base in the Black Sea. The Light Brigade charged,
the thin red line held, Florence Nightingale battered the army
medical services into shape, and the Treaty of Paris (1856) laid
down terms which could not be observed for long: the integrity
of the Ottoman Empire, the neutrality of the Black Sea, the good
treatment of the Sultan's Christian subjects. The next year saw
the Indian Mutiny which led, after much gallantry and brutality
on each side, to the wind-up of the East India Company and the
assumption by the government of responsibility for the affairs
of the sub-continent. Other peoples' wars achieved Italian
Liberation (1859–61), the abolition of slavery and preservation
of the United States of America (1861–65) and the creation of
the German Empire (1864- 65, 1866, 1870–71). Ministries led by
Palmerston, Disraeli, Russell and Gladstone avoided participa-
tion in these, though sometimes narrowly. In 1875 Disraeli scored
a dramatic imperial coup by buying a large holding of Suez
Canal shares. Once again the "unspeakable Turk" persecuted

Photograph by Ursula Hamilton

The Albert Memorial, Asia

his Christian subjects, Mr Gladstone thundered about Bulgarian atrocities, Russia and Turkey fought (1877–78) and Disraeli, incidentally acquiring control of Cyprus, brought back "Peace with Honour" from the Congress of Berlin. At home, after the Reform Acts of 1867 and 1884, pretty well every householder enjoyed the vote (with the blessing of a secret ballot since 1872), while Forster's Education Act of 1870 made elementary education universally available. The Queen, who retired with her grief for some time after the Prince Consort's death (1861), emerged again to the triumphs of her two jubilees. That of 1897 was deliberately planned to celebrate the greatness of Empire. With the picture of a formidable old lady, driving in magnificence to St. Paul's Cathedral, the image of a globe, plentifully adorned with red, floats before the mind's eye. A rash of islands in the Pacific, Atlantic and Indian Oceans; Gibraltar, Malta and Cyprus in the

Mediterranean; Canada, a Dominion since 1867; British Guiana; great tracts of West Africa, territory – British owned or controlled – almost all the way from the Cape to Cairo; India (Victoria had been Empress since 1877), Burma, Singapore, Hong-Kong; Australia and New Zealand, soon to be Commonwealth and Dominion respectively. Here lay the fruits of mighty achievements by Arnoldian schoolboys and Kiplingesque soldiers – yet, away in South Africa, we were soon to fight the Boers (1899–1902), a subject which will be discussed under the next reign.

When Queen Victoria died in January 1901 a whole age passed. Enormous changes had taken place like the urbanization of Britain and a rise of population from about 25 million to something like 41 million, but a monarchy which had been discredited was now felt to be not only a symbol but part and parcel of the life of the people and of the Empire, even if, save in rare cases, it had become politically powerless.

TWENTIETH CENTURY

1901–1983

Edward VII	1901–1910
George V	1910–1936
Edward VIII	1936
George VI	1936–1952
Elizabeth II	1952–

TWENTIETH CENTURY
Castrol House
(By permission of Gollins, Melvin, Ward and Partners)
(Gordon Fraser postcard)

TWENTIETH CENTURY

1901–1983

The twentieth century is one of unparalleled architectural opportunity owing to technical advance, efficient transport, and very wide variety of material. These factors have enabled architects to strike out in entirely new directions, unhampered by tradition, and the layman has found it hard to catch up. The main trends have been towards simplicity, even austerity and, more recently, "brutalism"; the reliance on form rather than ornamentation as in the Victorian period; and the use of framed buildings with thin outer skins rather than solid walls. And yet the century has seen plenty of revival too, especially in its early years, and Osbert Lancaster's expressions "Edwardian Baroque", "Stockbroker's Tudor", "Banker's Georgian" and "By-pass Variegated" eloquently describe some of its results.

Edward VII, by Sir Luke Fildes

(By permission of the National Portrait Gallery)

EDWARD VII, 1901–1910

(Son of VICTORIA and Prince Albert of Saxe-Coburg-Gotha)

Born 1841, was 59 when he ascended the throne, and 68 when he died.

Married Alexandra of Denmark, and had two sons:
    Albert, Duke of Clarence
    GEORGE V

and three daughters: Princess Louise Victoria Alexandra Dagmar, who married the Duke of Fife; Princess Victoria Alexandra Olga Mary; and Princess Maud Charlotte Mary Victoria, who married the King of Norway.

Thumbnail Sketch Over-disciplined in youth, and under-employed in manhood, Edward sought compensation in the fashionable round of a fast society. Nevertheless his geniality and dignity enabled him to popularize the Crown.

WHAT TO REMEMBER

Edward VII inherited not only a great Empire, but also the South African War (1899–1902). The Boers of the Transvaal, who had been guaranteed a wide degree of autonomy after their defeat of the British at Majuba Hill in 1881, were rendered uneasy by the grandiose schemes of Cecil Rhodes, Prime Minister of the Cape, and Chairman of the British South Africa Company—an odd mixture of saint and filibuster. Gold was discovered in their territory in 1886, and British fortune hunters flocked to the area where Johannesburg now stands. These foreigners ("Uitlanders"), enjoying no political rights but providing President Kruger's government with considerable fiscal profit, had a genuine "No-taxation-without-representation" problem, which they attempted to solve by rebellion, assisted from without by the abortive Jameson raid of 1895. Rhodes' complicity in this fiasco necessitated his resignation, Kaiser William II of Germany sent Kruger a congratulatory telegram, and the President prepared for war. During 2½ years we plodded through failure to an eventual methodically won victory. We were generous in the rehabilitation of the Boer Farmers, restored self-government to the Transvaal and her ally the Orange Free State in 1906, with the result that in 1910 the Union of South Africa could come into being.

The world at large had had little sympathy with Great Britain during these hostilities and, amongst our many critics, none spoke louder than William II of Germany, a monarch heartily disliked by his uncle Edward VII. Imperial Germany was becoming exceedingly powerful. A matchless army was now supported by a growing fleet, rendered the more formidable by the opening of the Kiel Canal in 1895. The Kaiser suffered from every sort of ambition – military, naval, colonial – and his great people, over-conscious of their distinguished gifts and qualities (and proud of their steel production), brooded enviously on the misfortune of having started late in the race for power. Germany was strengthened by The Triple Alliance, into which she had entered with Austria and Italy, over against which stood a Dual Alliance of Russia and France. England's "splendid isolation" was now clearly anachronistic, and we stepped out of it into the Anglo-Japanese Alliance of 1902. With Germany jealous and contemptuous, our next move was towards France. Agreement was reached over British interests in Egypt and those of the French in Morocco, "Good King Teddy" (as the Music Hall song had it) beamed genially upon the citizens of Paris, and the

informal but invaluable 'Entente Cordiale' of 1904 came into being. The very next year the Kaiser landed at Tangier and made a speech of some offensiveness because of French activities at Fez, which led to the resignation of the French Foreign Secretary and the compromise of the Algeciras Conference (1906), during which we stood by France. In 1907 we turned to Russia, no longer so menacing after her rough handling by Japan in the war of 1904–5, and a Triple Entente (Great Britain, Russia, France) was achieved. But Austria, backed by Germany, was powerful enough to seize Bosnia and Herzegovina in 1908, the Czar's protests proving vain.

Photograph by A. W. Kerr

Altar, Eton College Chapel. The redecoration of the East end of Eton College Chapel was part of the memorial to Old Etonians who fell in the South African War.

While the powers were thus regrouping and moving towards the disaster of 1914, life was not uneventful at home. Educational facilities were extended and made the responsibility of local authorities, and the ancient Free Trade battle was joined again in an attempt to protect British industries, with preferential treatment for Empire products. This brought down the Unionist Balfour ministry (the Unionists were Conservatives combined with such Liberals as opposed Gladstone's policy of Home Rule for Ireland) and put in a strong Liberal government (1906) under Sir Henry Campbell-Bannerman, whose mantle was to fall on Mr Asquith two years later. Sir Edward Grey was at the Foreign Office, R. B. Haldane started to prepare the country for major war, David Lloyd George, Chancellor of the Exchequer in 1908, produced his famous People's Budget in 1909, before a House which contained 50 Labour M.P.s, a formidable new political force. This budget, which struck at the wealthy and the landed proprietors in the cause of social reform, was thrown out by the House of Lords. After a dissolution and General Election the Peers wisely changed their tune and accepted it, but the Government was preparing a measure to curtail the power of the Upper House when Edward VII died.

George V, by Sir Oswald Birley
(*By permission of the National Portrait Gallery*)

GEORGE V, 1910–1936

(Son of EDWARD VII and Alexandra of Denmark)

Born 1865, was 44 when he ascended the throne, and 70 when he died.

Married Mary of Teck, and had five sons:

EDWARD VIII	Henry, Duke of Gloucester
GEORGE VI	George, Duke of Kent
Prince John, who died in childhood	

and one daughter: Princess Mary

Thumbnail Sketch A simple, dignified family man with a deep sense of duty and a genius for projecting himself by broadcast to nation and Commonwealth.

WHAT TO REMEMBER

A general election late in 1910 kept Mr Asquith in power but, as in the previous January, his majority in the Commons was achieved only with the assistance of Labour members and Irish members. The Parliament Bill was now passed (1911), the Upper House yielding before the threat of a mass creation of Liberal peers. No longer might the Lords reject a money bill, nor might they delay other legislation for more than two years. Mr Asquith now turned to reward his Irish allies with the Home Rule Bill of 1911, a measure obstructed by the Lords until 1914, when for a spell the Irish problem was shelved. Despite the passing of the National Insurance Act (1911), to the great benefit of the working man, these were bitter years. The constitutional crisis which George V had faced was symptomatic of profound social change. There was class rancour, there were strikes, suffragettes made courageous if irresponsible demonstrations, but in August 1914 the turbulent ranks closed against the enemy.

The continent of Europe presented no peaceful scene. German gestures continued, war flickered in the Balkans and, on 28 June 1914, a Serbian nationalist shot the Archduke Franz Ferdinand, heir to the Austro-Hungarian Empire, at Sarajevo, capital of the recently annexed Austrian province of Bosnia. Austria, determined to smash Serbian expansionist nationalism, presented, with Germany's support, an unacceptable ultimatum, to which Belgrade made a conciliatory reply. This went unheeded in Vienna, despite Germany's last-minute attempt to apply the brake. On 28 July Austria declared war on Serbia, Russia mobilized on Serbia's behalf, on 1 August Germany declared war on Russia and, on 3 August, on Russia's ally France. England joined France and Russia on 4 August, as a result of the violation of Belgian neutrality.

And so the lamps went out all over Europe, and the long way to Tipperary led through Mons, Ypres, Gallipoli, Jutland, the Somme and Passchendaele to Marshal Foch's railway coach at Compiègne, where an Armistice was signed (11 November 1918).

At the Treaty of Versailles (1919) the New World idealism of President Wilson's Fourteen Points (America had intervened decisively on the allies' side in 1917) faded before Clemenceau's ruthless European realism – even Wilson's League of Nations came into being without the U.S.A. Severe terms were imposed on Germany of which, perhaps, the war-guilt clause, the occupation and demilitarization of the Rhineland, and the creation of the Polish Corridor were most resented. In Munich a maladjusted corporal, who had found fulfilment on the Western Front,

brooded darkly. The Eastern Baltic coastline saw a crop of new republics, and the Treaty of Saint Germain achieved the disintegration of the Austrian Empire, putting unfamiliar names such as Czechoslovakia and Jugoslavia on the map.

Throughout the world, belligerents tried to rehabilitate themselves. In Britain Lloyd George, war-winning coalition Premier, gave the vote to all men over 21 and all women over 30. In 1922 Mr Bonar-Law replaced him with a Conservative ministry. Ireland battled from the Easter Rebellion of 1916, through the troubles of Sinn Fein, the Black and Tans,

Rima, by Epstein
(By courtesy of Mr Hans Wild)

the Free State (1921), the Civil War (1922–3), to the loosing of official bonds achieved by Mr de Valera. Mr Baldwin succeeded Mr Bonar Law from 1923 to 1924 and, with a short interval for the first Labour government of Mr Ramsay Macdonald (1924), was in again until 1929. Post-war economic troubles were severe and industrial unrest reached its peak with the General Strike of 1926. In 1928 all men and women over 21 acquired the vote, and the continued rise of the Labour Party was demonstrated by Mr Macdonald's return to power in 1929. A world slump and Britain's financial crisis resulted in a National Government (1931), first under the leadership of Macdonald, and subsequently (1935) of Baldwin. The Statute of Westminster (1931) defined the position of this country and the Dominions within the British Commonwealth of Nations, economic conditions improved and, by 1935, when George V drove to St. Paul's Cathedral after 25 years on the throne, a feeling of thankfulness and cautious optimism was abroad.

But in Europe, despite the cameraderie of Locarno (1925) and the idealism of the Kellogg Pact (1928), shadows were falling. Mussolini and Hitler had come to power, nationalists for whom war was still the legitimate continuation of policy. When George V died in January 1936, Hitler had denounced the Treaty of Versailles and Mussolini's Abyssinian adventure was in full swing.

Edward VIII

(By permission of Radio Times, Hulton Picture Library)

EDWARD VIII, 1936

(Son of GEORGE V and Mary of Teck)

Born 1894, was 41 when he ascended the throne, and 42 when he abdicated.

Unmarried, whilst on the throne.

Thumbnail Sketch A versatile man of brilliant promise, whose abdication saddened a bewildered people.

WHAT TO REMEMBER

The sad, uneasy reign of this uncrowned king saw Hitler's descent upon the Rhineland, Mussolini's capture of Addis Ababa, civil war in Spain and Edward's determination to marry Mrs Wallis Simpson, whose two previous marriages had been dissolved in the courts, a resolve which led inevitably to his abdication.

On the night of 11 December 1936, Edward VIII, by then "H.R.H. Prince Edward", broadcast as follows:

"At long last I am able to say a few words of my own. I have never wanted to withhold anything, but until now it has not been constitutionally possible for me to speak.

A few hours ago I discharged my last duty as King and Emperor, and now I have been succeeded by my brother, the Duke of York, my first words must be to declare my allegiance to him. This I do with all my heart.

You all know the reasons which have impelled me to renounce the Throne. But I want you to understand that in making up my mind I did not forget the country or the Empire which, as Prince of Wales, and lately as King, I have for twenty-five years tried to serve. But you must believe me when I tell you that I have found it impossible to carry the heavy burden of responsibility and to discharge my duties as King as I would wish to do without the help and support of the woman I love.

And I want you to know that the decision I have made has been mine and mine alone. This was a thing I had to judge entirely for myself. The other person most nearly concerned has tried up to the last to persuade me to take a different course. I have made this, the most serious decision of my life, upon a single thought of what would, in the end, be best for all.

This decision has been made less difficult for me by the sure knowledge that my Brother, with his long training in the public affairs of this country, and with his fine qualities, will be able to take my place forthwith, without interruption or injury to the life and progress of the Empire. And he has one matchless blessing, enjoyed by so many of you and not bestowed on me – a happy home with his wife and children.

During these hard days I have been comforted by my Mother and by my Family. The Ministers of the Crown, and in particular Mr Baldwin, the Prime Minister, have always treated me with full consideration. There has never been any constitutional difference between me and them and between me and Parliament. Bred in the constitutional tradition by my Father, I should never have allowed any such issue to arise.

Ever since I was Prince of Wales, and later on when I occupied the Throne, I have been treated with the greatest kindness by all classes, wherever I have lived or journeyed throughout the Empire. For that I am very grateful.

I now quit altogether public affairs, and I lay down my burden. It may be some time before I return to my native land, but I shall always follow the fortunes of the British race

and Empire with profound interest, and if at any time in the future I can be found of service to His Majesty in a private station, I shall not fail.

And now we all have a new King. I wish him, and you, his people, happiness and prosperity with all my heart. God bless you. God Save the King."

At 2 a.m. on 12 December 1936 the destroyer "Fury" bore away from Portsmouth the much-travelled Prince, who will be remembered by many with gratitude for the days when he was known as "Britain's First Ambassador".

Photograph by Ursula Hamilton

Coronation Goblet

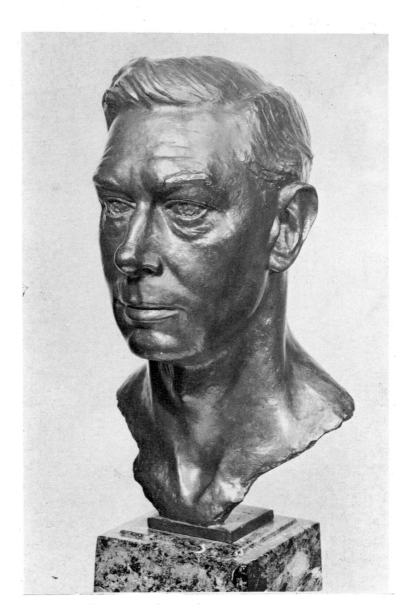

George VI, Bronze by Sir William Reid Dick
(*By permission of the National Portrait Gallery*)

GEORGE VI, 1936–1952

(Son of GEORGE V and Mary of Teck.
Brother of EDWARD VIII)

Born 1895, was 40 when he ascended the throne, and 56 when he died.

Married Lady Elizabeth Bowes-Lyon, and had two daughters:
ELIZABETH II
Princess Margaret

Thumbnail Sketch He had greatness thrust upon him, and gave an admirable example of how a man should do his duty.

WHAT TO REMEMBER

The reign thus thrust upon George VI was to be one of the most momentous in our history. The immediate preoccupations were with Foreign Policy. Neville Chamberlain succeeded Baldwin in 1937 and, faced by a new and sinister line-up, the Berlin-Rome-Tokyo "Axis", did his best to appease its members' power hunger. Hitler's rearmament was proceeding apace and, on 11 March 1938, he annexed Austria. With remorseless logic he then turned to Czechoslovakia, which he had outflanked, and within whose frontiers resided some 9 million Sudeten Germans. By mid September 1938 it seemed that Hitler was going to take the Sudetenland by force and, on the fifteenth of that month, Chamberlain flew off to the historic interview at Berchtesgaden. Meetings followed at Godesberg on 23 September and finally at Munich on the 29th, when Mussolini and Daladier, the French premier, were also present. The outcome was that Germany acquired the Sudeten areas, while Czechoslovakia had to be content with unimpressive promises guaranteeing the integrity of her remaining territory. Back in London Chamberlain was unwise enough to quote Disraeli, and claim the achievement of "Peace with Honour".

In 1939 Führer Hitler returned to the inexorable prosecution of his plans. In March he seized the whole of Czechoslovakia and, as a sideline, Memel. The baleful German spotlight now illuminated Poland, and Chamberlain, in a moment of truth, promised assistance if Polish independence were threatened. Hitler was demanding Danzig and railway access across the famous corridor to East Prussia and Memel. On 23 August there came the dreaded and decisive news that Germany and the U.S.S.R. had made an alliance, after which all communications and interviews were farcical, for the Nazis palpably wanted war. Poland was invaded on 1 September 1939 and, at 11 a.m. on 3 September, Germany was once again our foe. An air-raid siren wailed and the trench-diggers girded themselves resignedly, realizing that this would be a different kind of struggle, for much had happened since the brothers Wright flew their heavier-than-air machine in 1903, and Von Richthofen engaged in chivalrous combat on the Western front from 1916 to 1918.

World War II is alive in many memories: the martyrdom of Poland, the agony of France, the Battle of Britain, the Blitz, Hitler's ill-judged march on Moscow, Pearl Harbour, the meetings of Churchill, Roosevelt and Stalin, the Western Desert, Burma, the Pacific, D-Day, the V.1 and V.2, the Berlin Bunker and Germany's unconditional surrender on 7 May 1945. There are names of defeat: Dunkirk and Singapore; names of glory: Alamein, Stalingrad and Kohima; names of horror: Hiroshima and Nagasaki; names of shame: Belsen, Buchenwald and Auschwitz. As far as Britain was concerned, behind all effort, and over all policy, was Winston Churchill, directing this life and

death struggle with a gusto derived from the tough glories of England's history. He made us all conscious of this. We have been good and bad, sincere and hypocritical, industrious and idle, ruthless and sentimental, brave and cowardly, but we have seldom been defeated. Because of Churchill many of his countrymen and countrywomen are thankful to have been adults between 1939 and 1945.

It was probably the state discipline and state planning to which they had become accustomed during nearly six years which led the British people to accept Mr Attlee's socialist government in July 1945. They also accepted U.N.O., austerity, a considerable degree of nationalization, Lord Mount-

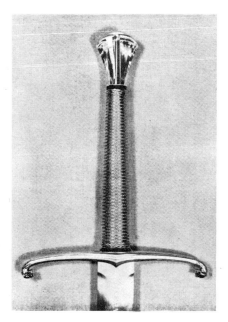

The Sword of Honour for Stalingrad, designed by
R. M. Y. Gleadowe
(*By courtesy of* The Studio)

battory whirlwind, viceroyalty (whereby India and Pakistan were created and we withdrew from the sub-continent), National Health and N.A.T.O. They engaged in the Korean War. There was, too, a realization of the great shift of Western power to America, of the vital importance of Anglo-American relations, and of the need to develop atomic energy, not only in order to have a strong voice in the affairs of a world in which peace is being kept by a balance of terror, but because we cannot live on coal for all time.

The election of October 1951 brought Churchill back and, on 6 February 1952, George VI died. He had served his peoples for just over fifteen tremendous years with unfaltering gallantry, and had not hesitated, in the final event, to sacrifice his health to the demands with which Great Britain burdens the wearer of her crown.

Elizabeth II, by Edward Halliday

(*By courtesy of the Auckland Institute and Museum, Auckland, New Zealand*)

ELIZABETH II, 1952–

(Daughter of His late Majesty King GEORGE VI and of Her Majesty Queen Elizabeth the Queen Mother)

Born 1926, was 25 when she ascended the throne.

Married H.R.H. the Prince Philip, Duke of Edinburgh, and has four children:

> H.R.H. The Prince of Wales, married Lady Diana Spencer.
> H.R.H. Princess Anne Elizabeth Alice Louise, married Captain Mark Phillips.
> H.R.H. Prince Andrew Albert Christian Edward.
> H.R.H. Prince Edward Anthony Richard Louis.

Thumbnail Sketch THE QUEEN; GOD BLESS HER.

WHAT TO REMEMBER

All periods, of course, are ages of transition. But one may be pardoned for thinking that the winds of change have blown with greater force and driven the mills of history to turn at greater speed between 1952 and 1982 than in many other spans of thirty years. Today, as Britons look back upon crises in Kenya, Malaya, Suez, Cyprus, Rhodesia and Northern Ireland, the country is still studying its new part on the world's stage – a part forced upon it by a diminution of power, the loss of an Empire, and subtle changes in the Commonwealth. Furthermore, reaction from the austere discipline of the war years, to some extent preserved until 1956 by National Service, has given birth to what many choose to call "The Permissive Society" – and a country which comparatively lately believed it had "never had it so good" now grapples with the problems of unemployment, industrial unrest and inflation.

Yet the situation could be even more difficult were it not for the personality and popularity of the reigning Queen. At the time of her accession Elizabeth II was 25 years old. She had married H.R.H. the Prince Philip, Duke of Edinburgh, in 1947 and had given birth to two children: H.R.H. the Prince of Wales, married in 1981 to Lady Diana Spencer, and H.R.H. Princess Anne, married in 1973 to Captain Mark Phillips. At the time of her Silver Jubilee (1977) Her Majesty was 51 and the family included two more sons.

It has been said that "the English dearly love a Lord", but a blind loyalty to established institutions would hardly be characteristic of later twentieth-century democracy. Nevertheless the Silver Jubilee, followed in 1981 by the magic of what we shall no doubt, for many years, continue to call "The Royal Wedding", demonstrated the fact that this closely-knit family commands genuine admiration and real affection both in the British Isles and further afield, the more so since the Prince and Princess of Wales now have a son.

Even so the eight Prime Ministers who have served Queen Elizabeth II have clearly been beset by a more than normal share of the anxieties and problems which their office brings. And here, especially, it is important to remember that the monarchy is an institution of enormous practical value.

Walter Bagehot, in 1867, saw the British ruler as a figure to be consulted, to give encouragement and, where necessary, to give warning. To fulfil this function the wearers of the British crown need a capacity for hard work (the grind of the dispatch boxes is ceaseless) and an intelligence which can cope with the daily flood of information. Cleverness, as such, is not necessary, but good sense and sound judgment are vital – and these qualities her subjects believe their present Queen to have in abundance.

And so the Commonwealth may now pause for a moment to take stock. Much of that great area (more than ten million square miles) has been visited by the Queen; many of its inhabitants

(over nine hundred and fifty millions) have seen her; of fifteen of the forty-five member countries she is Head of State. Vastly travelled, she has, naturally, greatly increased in confidence and now performs all that is demanded of her not only with a natural charm but also with the assurance of a professional.

The Rocking Chair, by Henry Moore
(*By courtesy of Mrs Irina Moore*)

INDEX